Saga of the Samurai: Book 1

TAKEDA RISES TO POWER

THE KAI TAKEDA 1 (1130-1467)

Terje Solum · Anders K. Rue

Brookhurst Press

First Edition

Copyright © 2003 by Brookhurst Press

All rights reserved. No part of this book may be reproduced or used in any form or by any means including but not limited to graphic, cyberspace, electronic, or mechanical, or for any use as an information storage and retrieval system, without written permission from Brookhurst Press.

Printed by Creative Press, Anaheim, CA
Edited By Dan Weber
Translated By Ian Harkness
Weapon Illustrations & Maps By Jan B. Loa
Designed By Creative Pull, Ananheim, CA

Brookhurst Press
12188 Brookhurst St.
Garden Grove, CA 92840

Phone (714) 636-3580
Fax (714) 636-9150

E-mail: info@sagaofthesamurai.com

Web Site:
www.sagaofthesamurai.com

Title Page Photograph

Kôfu valley as seen from Mount Atago.
Mount Fuji is visible in the background.

DEDICATION

To my Chen Hsiu Yu

ACKNOWLEDGEMENTS

I am extremely grateful to the book's illustrator, Anders K. Rue, for his excellent drawings, and Jan B. Loa who drew the weapon illustrations and maps. I also wish to express my thanks to Henry Tremblay and his staff at Brookhurst Hobbies for all their assistance. I am deeply indebted to my Japanese family in Tokyo, who have kindly opened the door of their home to me over a period of several years. Their kind hospitality has enabled me to visit Japan and study the country's history.

NOTES ON THE TEXT

The Japanese names in the book are written surname first, in accordance with tradition. Japanese vowels will sometimes be distinguished with a diacritical mark, '^.' This indicates that the vowel is twice as long. This has been done to differentiate between certain family names, such as Môri and Mori, and to facilitate pronunciation. In addition, to avoid confusion, the terms "family" and "clan" are used interchangeably throughout the book. Lastly, unless stated otherwise, the dates are in keeping with the old Japanese calendar.

Terje Solum has for more than a decade studied the history of Japan, specializing in the Sengoku Jidai period. In addition to having studied the Japanese language at an institute near Nagoya, he has traveled all over Japan in search of infomation related to the samurai. *Saga of the Samurai* is his first major book project.

Anders K. Rue is a commercial artist living and working in Norway. Working within a wide range of styles, for the last 5 years he has concentrated on drawings recreating historical events. His best known art is found in the the book *The Kings of Norway* and a newly published version of *Snorre*, the epic saga of the Vikings.

photo TAK 1-1

The statue of Takeda Shingen in front of Kôfu station, Kôfu city.

INTRODUCTION

In the beginning, the Emperor and his family ruled Japan. The need for warriors to protect the Emperor and his family had been a necessity since the time of the first Emperor, Jinmu. From the earliest days of invasion, the Japanese were at war with the natives of the Japanese islands, the Ainu. The Japanese were in constant need of more and more land, and the Ainu stood in their way. Gradually warriors that fought near the border to Ainu lands became permanent dwellers, and the so-called 'true warrior families' were born. These people lived in a state of constant war with their neighbors, and it was here that *bushidô*, or 'the way of the warrior' began.

Daily training with several kinds of weapons on foot and horseback made these warrior families into what we see them as today - fearsome warriors. Over time, the samurai took more and more land that had belonged to the Ainu, and through the centuries these samurai warrior houses became a force to be reckoned with. Some of the most powerful families, like the Fujiwara, Abe, and Taira families, were in close contact with the Emperor and his Court and became a part of the administrative machinery. In fact many of the warrior houses were descendants from the Imperial family. Those Imperial family members not in line to be Emperor founded their own families; families that later became the warrior houses of Japan.

By the beginning of the 10th century many powerful samurai families had started to fight amongst themselves and gradually the Emperor lost his control over the samurai. It all came to a head in the 12th century when two major families, the Taira and Minamoto, went to war with one another (1180-1185). When the 'Genpei War' was over and the Minamoto clan was left as victor their leader, Minamoto Yoritomo, was appointed *Shôgun* by the Emperor in 1192. In doing so the Emperor gave command of the army and total political power to the Minamoto. Yoritomo's actions left the Emperor little choice. After that, samurai ruled Japan, and they would do so until 1868 when political power was returned to the Imperial House.

One of the most exciting periods in this time of samurai was the so-called *Sengoku Jidai*, or 'The Age of the Country at War' (1467-1615). Over a period of 150 years, thousands of battles were fought within the country, destroying the fortunes of hundreds of families. A fortunate few succeeded beyond their wildest dreams, laying claim to more territory than they had ever been able to before. With the outbreak of the Ônin War in 1467, the Ashikaga *Shogunate* began its decline. The word *Shogunate* can be translated as Military Regime, but the literal translation is General of the Army. The war ended in 1477, leaving in its wake a lawless society with no effective central government. As a result, more than a century after

photo TAK 1-2

Since the first people came to Kai province, sacred Mount Fuji has been their guardian.

its rise to power in 1338 the Ashikaga family was gradually losing its hold on the country. Although the Ashikaga family continued to hold positions of prestige for another century, their influence during that time was nominal. As their authority declined, power fell into the hands of local clans that took little heed of Ashikaga's edicts. Though these families ruled with little interference from the central authorities, they soon began to squabble with their neighbors over ownership of the land. This led to a state of nearly constant warfare between these clans. The confrontations did not subside until the battle of Osaka in 1615, when Tokugawa Ieyasu crushed the last serious contender to the title of *Shôgun*. This victory was followed by almost 250 years of unbroken peace.

This is the first volume in a series on the leading Samurai families of this time. In this book, we will explore the early history of the Takeda family of Kai Province. In the West, this aristocratic clan is best known for its charismatic and able leader, Takeda Shingen, who lived during the sixteenth century. The general history of the Takeda clan, however, is little known outside of Japan. On several occasions during its 600-year history the family teetered on the brink of extinction. The Takeda family was often forced to resolve conflicts with enemies both inside and outside their borders by force of arms. This first volume will describe the struggle of the clan to maintain its influence, from the first Takeda to the beginning of the Ônin War in 1467. This thrilling epic spans over 500 years of history. In this book, we will become acquainted with members of the Takeda clan who played decisive roles in the family's early history, and touch upon significant events that influenced their lives.

Ch. 1 – The Origins of the Takeda Family

THE MINAMOTO CLAN

During the turbulent years of the 11th and 12th centuries, the Minamoto clan successively vanquished their adversaries: the Abe, Kiyohara, Fujiwara and Taira families. They eventually became the uncontested rulers of Honshû, the largest island in Japan. In order to understand how they subjugated the leading families of Japan and rose to power, we must examine the historical backdrop that allowed these conquests to take place.

The Minamoto were a typical warrior clan. Because of this, aristocratic families close to the Emperor's Court, such as the Taira and Fujiwara families, regarded the Minamoto from the east as vulgar and unrefined. They lacked the social network and concerns of the aristocracy, who were mostly interested in administration, poetry, literature, the arts and games. The Minamoto, on the other hand, preferred to study martial arts, which they used to enforce their policies, crush rebellions and ensure peace and order. Although the Minamoto had chosen the military as a way of life, they were also fully aware of the importance of remaining on good terms with the right people, especially the Emperor and his Court.

THE ABE, KIYOHARA AND FUJIWARA CLANS

After decades of strife in central Honshû, the northern clans had become accustomed to doing as they pleased, and several had accrued considerable military and political power. These families were mostly concerned with local issues, and were not particularly interested in conflicts that did not affect them. After permitting several years of this type of autonomy, the central government attempted to re-establish its authority in the north. When the northern clans chose to openly ignore direct orders from the capital, their fate was sealed. Minamoto Yoriyoshi was appointed by the central government to subdue the unruly Abe clan in the Tôhoku region of northern Japan, where the Kiyohara clan also held power. This marked the beginning of the Early Nine-Years' War (1051-1062).

The Abe clan had managed to build a substantial army over the years, and proved to be a formidable opponent; but a large army does not guarantee success without competent leadership. In this regard, the Minamoto clan had the advantage. They were accomplished in the military arts, and preferred the sword to the word in the solution of conflicts. After many years of warfare, the clan's generals were also experienced strategists. The Abe clan was doomed the moment the Minamoto accepted the task of meeting them in battle. In 1062, following engagements at Koromogawa, Toriumi and Kuriyagawa, the Abe clan was defeated. Though the clan continued to exist, it never fully recovered, and retained little of its former influence.

With the defeat of the Abe clan, the Fujiwara and Kiyohara clans saw an opportunity to expropriate some of the Abe lands and extend their political and military influence in the north. They were mostly interested in acquiring cultivated land. The vast majority of wars fought during the Japanese Middle Ages involved cultivated land, especially paddy fields.

Although the Fujiwara and Kiyohara clans benefited from the fate of the Abe clan, they did not view the Abe's fate as purely positive. Realizing it was only a matter of time before their actions came to the attention of the Emperor they took the necessary precautions. Both clans fortified their borders, concentrating their troops at strategic points to guard the most important access roads. These troops could provide strong opposition to any military power foolhardy enough to attempt an invasion. Likewise, political power was as essential as military might. The Fujiwara clan, unlike the Abe, had strong political influence, especially at the Court of the Emperor in Kyôto. This political influence ensured that the Minamoto would have met strong resistance at court if a battle had broken out between themselves and the Fujiwara clan.

photo TAK 1-3

Kamanashi River. Further to the north lies Suwa in Shinano Province. In this picture the river is deceptively peaceful; almost every year this river became the villain of the valley when it overflowed its banks.

Before the Minamoto could take steps against the Fujiwara clan a new task emerged. The entire northern region was now subject to discord and disorder, with several branches of the powerful Kiyohara clan embroiled in armed conflicts. This unrest came about when the Kiyohara and several of their branch families started to quarrel over land and local power. The Kiyohara clan was blamed for instigating the unrest, forcing the government in Kyôto to react. Even the Kiyohara clan's political influence could not deter the Emperor. A punitive expedition under the leadership of Minamoto Yoshiie was sent to subdue the Kiyohara. In a series of battles between 1083 and 1087, Yoshiie decimated the Kiyohara family and established the absolute sovereignty of the Minamoto in the north. These battles are collectively referred to as the Later Three-Years' War and restored peace in the Tôhoku area - at least temporarily. Despite their many military successes, the Minamoto were not alone in the north; the Fujiwara clan also remained an unyielding power in the region. It would not be until the end of the 12th century that the two powers would meet one another on the field of battle.

For their services in bringing order to the northern provinces, the Minamoto were rewarded with appointments to public office and assigned posts in areas where they had defeated enemies of the central government. These appointments were common rewards during the period. The Minamoto became responsible for the administration of the provinces or districts, and were expected to enforce peace, and ensure that the region was economically productive.

SHINRASABURÔ YOSHIMITSU AND KAI PROVINCE

One of the generals who took part in the punitive expedition against the Kiyohara was Shinrasaburô Yoshimitsu. He was the third son of Minamoto Yoriyoshi, and participated in each battle during the Later Three-Years' War. A skilful warrior with great courage, and renowned for his exploits, Yoshimitsu was rewarded with appointments for his successes during the war.

photo TAK 1-4 & 1-5

The Fuefuki (1-4) and Kamanashi (1-5) were the two main rivers in Kôfu valley, but it was the Fuefuki that caused the majority of trouble for the Takeda during the time they lived at Isawa.

When a young samurai reached 15 years of age, he underwent a ceremony called *genpuku*, the "coming of age" ritual. Although 15 was the typical age for the *genpuku* ritual, samurai between 12 and 17 often participated in the ceremony. Some sources tell of boys as young as 5 or 6 years of age being initiated during the Tokugawa *Shogunate*, which governed during the Edo period (1603-1867). When a boy had taken the step into the world of the adults, he was allowed to wear the characteristic hair bun, a distinguishing sign of a samurai. The more famous half-moon shaved haircut of the samurai did not come into practice until the 15th century. After the ceremony the young samurai was presented with a suit of armor made especially for him. He would also receive a new name during the ceremony. It usually consisted of two Chinese characters, one of which was hereditary. In addition, permission was granted to use part of a lord's name; in some cases it was typical to use one of the two characters that made up the name of the *Shôgun*. The name *Yoshimitsu* can be traced back to his *genpuku* ceremony, held at the Onjôji temple in Ômi Province. The ceremony was held under the protection of the god Shiragi Myôjin. Yoshimitsu acquired his name, Shinrasaburô, under the auspices of Shiragi. Saburô stands for "the third son" and was a commonly used suffix.

TAK 1-4

TAK 1-5

Minamoto Yoshimitsu was rewarded with the title *Kai no Kami* (Lord of Kai), while he simultaneously held the title *Hitachi no Kami* (Lord of Hitachi). After the Later Three-Years' War, Yoshimitsu settled in the province of Kai, and according to early sources, moved to a village called Wakamiko. It is reported that he built a manor called Wakamiko Castle there. The title, Lord of Kai, was first awarded to his grandfather, Yorinobu, around 1030, then to his father, Yoriyoshi, and finally to Yoshimitsu.

Today, the former Kai Province is known as the Yamanashi Prefecture. It consists largely of a long valley, running approximately 92 kilometers north to south and 80 kilometers east to west, bordered by two mountain chains. In the southern part of Kôfu valley is a large rectangular region encircled by mountains, crisscrossed by a few rivers. It was in this valley the family that would become known as the Takeda settled. The area is about 70 kilometers northwest of Tôkyô, as the bird flies. Kai is an inland province, and in July and August the heat and humidity are almost tropical in character. In the winter, the heavy snowfall and cold made military campaigns impractical, and warfare was, therefore, largely seasonal in nature. The agricultural areas produced products such as rice, fruit, cotton, and silk. Raw materials from the region were frequently used in the production of paper, textiles, pottery, and similar export commodities. Another extremely lucrative activity was the breeding of quality horses. Over the centuries the Takeda produced a renowned line of steeds that was highly prized throughout Japan. The area was also rich in natural resources; including gold, lumber, and iron. Many of the resources were not extensively exploited prior to the 1500's. Commercial mining and production did not really take off until Takeda Nobutora and his son, Shingen, took over the administration of the area in the 16th century.

THE NAME TAKEDA AND TAKEDA KANJA

The Takeda family name has two possible derivations. Minamoto Yoshimitsu was the governor of Hitachi Province before he became *Kai no Kami*. The Takeda name quite possibly derives from his stay in Hitachi. One of Yoshimitsu's sons, Yoshinari, settled in a village called Satake. Another son, Yoshikiyo, moved to a village called Takeda in the Naka District. Both Satake and Takeda were located within Hitachi province. There he built a fort called Numao, which he used as his headquarters. While he lived there, he might have been referred to as Takeda *kanja* (*kanja* = young), though this title is not mentioned in official documents. Perhaps this is the origin of the family name; but several generations later one of his descendants,

photo TAK 1-6

Taken from Takeda Hachimangû, looking toward Mount Fuji (in the background).

Takeda Nobuyoshi, settled in a village of the same name, near Mount Amariyama in Kai. It is after this village that some Japanese historians believe that the Takeda surname first appears.

HEMI YOSHIKIYO

When Yoshimitsu died, his son Yoshikiyo became head of the clan. Yoshikiyo apparently claimed control of both Hitachi and Kai against the will of certain families in the Hitachi Province. This nearly resulted in armed revolt. Perhaps the situation was so unstable when Yoshikiyo assumed power that he had no possibility of re-establishing order and those families in opposition to his governance did not wish to see another Hemi in control regardless of whether or not Yoshikiyo could re-establish order. Whatever the cause, he was apparently unable to contain the continuing unrest, and was accused of total incompetence. The Imperial Court in Kyôto exiled him to Ichikawa, an insignificant village in the Kai Mountains. Being banished to Ichikawa apparently did not adversely affect Yoshikiyo's true ability to administrate. As soon as he was settled in his new fief, he began to take steps to increase productivity. He ordered his subordinates to clear land and create new rice paddies. Within a few years, he had improved the economic circumstances of everyone in his district. When he died in 1149, his grateful subjects raised a monument to honor his memory. He left behind a province in rapid economic expansion – a province that would require a wise and powerful successor to administrate. The challenge fell to his son, Kiyomitsu.

HEMI KIYOMITSU

Kiyomitsu was born in 1110, in the village of Takeda in Hitachi. After his failures in Hitachi and Kai, Kiyomitsu's father, Yoshikiyo, had regained his self-confidence, and in 1130 took his son to their new home in Ichikawa. When Kiyomitsu reached Ichikawa he did not linger, but instead moved away and started his own family. He chose to settle in a village called Hemi, north of Ichikawa. According to tradition, a new lord adopted the name of his new village when he moved from his parents hometown. Consequently, Kiyomitsu used Hemi as his surname, and was addressed as *Hemi kanja..*

photo TAK 1-7

Shows the mountains to the right of the Takeda Hachimangû. Lumber was not a problem in Kai, as all the hills and mountains in the valley were covered with trees.

Hemi Kiyomitsu's most significant feat was to build a network of roads within his domain. He did this in order to improve communication between the villages and fortresses of the district and facilitate the movement of cavalry. Kai Province had bred horses for centuries and was renowned for the speed and stamina of these magnificent animals. These horses were highly prized throughout the country and the lords of Kai sometimes gave them as gifts to the nobility and other leaders in return for services rendered. This could be regarded as a form of bribery (and was often just that). Kiyomitsu

photo TAK 1-8

Taken from the Takeda Hachiman Shrine in Nirasaki city. The shrine is said to have been built in 822, and for centuries it served the people and the Takeda clan.

photo TAK 1-9

This marker shows the location where Takeda Nobuyoshi's mansion stood. A few hundred meters up to the left in the picture is the famous Hachiman Shrine.

was also known for his insatiable appetite for women. His consorts were so numerous that he managed to father more than 30 children. His first-born son, Mitsunaga, was sickly from birth, and so it was his second son, Nobuyoshi, who inherited his title. Kiyomitsu participated in two major military campaigns in the 1150's: *Hôgen no ran* in 1156 and *Heiji no ran* in 1159. The clan from Kai sided with Minamoto Yoshitomo during these turbulent years, and its soldiers and generals fought well. Yoshitomo praised the Kai clan's efforts during this difficult time. Hemi Kiyomitsu died in 1168.

TAKEDA NOBUYOSHI

Nobuyoshi's father decided his son should move to another village called Takeda, near Mount Amariyama, and raise a family there. Nobuyoshi obediently summoned his family and personal vassals, and moved to Takeda. It is here that the famous holy temple of Takeda Hachiman, the Takeda war-god, stands. Nobuyoshi built his estate roughly 300 meters from the famous temple, and the ruins of his residence can still be seen today.

Nobuyoshi had several ambitious plans for his province, one of the most important being increasing rice production. To accomplish this, a large work force was conscripted to clear land and lay out rice paddies. As a result, rice fields sprang up quickly throughout the valley. Since rice was the most important source of nutrition in Japan, this gave Nobuyoshi a broad economic base with which to finance his other projects. One such undertaking was to organize a more systematic and consistent training program for his soldiers. For the samurai, daily training in archery from horseback (*yabusame*), spear (*yari*), and sword (*tachi*) fighting were stressed. Farmers, who served in the rural companies, or *kunishû*, were also trained. This emphasis on hard military training proved to be of great advantage to the family. During the following years, they had many opportunities to put their soldiers to the test.

Ch. 2 – The Genpei War

THE BEGINNING OF THE WAR

Nobuyoshi's greatest challenge took place in 1180, with the outbreak of the Genpei War. The name of this war is derived from the Chinese character *Gen*, which stands for the Minamoto clan, and *Hei*, which represents the Taira clan. These were two of the most powerful clans in Japan at the time. After several years of minor confrontations, the two families found themselves embroiled in a major war lasting almost five years. Yoritomo, the leader of the Minamoto family, enjoyed little success in his military efforts at the beginning of the war. His tiny army of 300 men engaged numerically superior forces under the combined leadership of Ôba Kagechika and his younger brother, Matano Kagehisa, near Ishibashiyama on the 23rd of August 1180. This battle resulted in a crushing defeat for Yoritomo, and he barely managed to escape over the Hakone Mountains with a few survivors. Not feeling safe even with the mountains to protect them, they continued on to a village on the coast, where Yoritomo's men commandeered a boat. Yoritomo and his forces finally found temporary refuge in Awa Province, far from the enemy.

Yoritomo realized that his position was hopeless if he could not find allies in the struggle against the Taira generals so he sought help from the Takeda family. Yoritomo chose his general Hôjô Tokimasa (1138-1215) to conduct negotiations with the Takeda. Tokimasa was an able general and politician, who had been an influential political leader on the Izu Peninsula for many years. Accompanied by his son, Yoshitoki, he went to Kai to meet with Nobuyoshi where he asked for Nobuyoshi's aid in his conflict with the Taira family. Nobuyoshi had anticipated this request, and was prepared to help. He had been in Kai at the time of the battle in Ishibashiyama, and had used the subsequent interlude to muster the Takeda clan's allies. Their soldiers had reported with full armor and weapons, prepared for battle. It took only Yoritomo's request for Nobuyoshi to join him in the campaign.

Ôba Kagechika was riding high on his victory over Yoritomo. In order to increase his advantage, he sent Matano Kagehisa with an army from Suruga Province to Tachibana Tômochi. Together, the two generals intended to invade Kai Province. Confident of victory, they marched on Nobuyoshi, whose *shinobi* (informers) kept him constantly informed of his enemies' movements. Nobuyoshi realized that he would soon meet worthy opponents, and tried to find a way to increase his chances for success. The armies of Nobuyoshi's adversaries camped at the foot of Mount Hashida and threw a boisterous sake party that evening, most likely prematurely celebrating their victory. Through his *shinobi*, Nobuyoshi got wind of the party, and it gave him an idea.

NOBUYOSHI'S INSPIRATION

With daybreak, a wave of unrest swept through the camp. The first soldiers who arose, each undoubtedly suffering from a hangover, found to their dismay that more than a hundred bowstrings had been severed. The bows would be useless until the strings were replaced. Matano Kagehisa woke from the disturbance, and was informed of the situation. The explanation for the severed bowstrings became obvious when the lookouts cried, "we're under attack!"

With thundering hooves, the Takeda cavalry charged into the main encampment. Half-naked soldiers tried in vain to organize some form of defense, but unarmed and virtually helpless, many were slaughtered by Nobuyoshi's cavalry. As the battle progressed, Matano's forces were pressed gradually back towards the foot of Mount Hashida. Soon the survivors were battling to simply survive. Some ran down the road or up the mountain to escape Nobuyoshi's cavalry. The slaughter continued until Nobuyoshi's soldiers were finally satisfied and returned to camp. It was a great victory for Nobuyoshi, and news of the Taira clan's defeat spread rapidly. Yoritomo and the military leadership were pleased with the victory. The *Shogun* badly needed a change in fortune. The optimism and fighting spirit of his men had suffered greatly from the defeat at Ishibashiyama a few months earlier. Both he and his men took courage from Nobuyoshi's victory. The battle also proved that the Taira generals were not invincible.

Nobuyoshi's simple but effective strategy undoubtedly saved the lives of many of his men. If his adversaries had been able to use their bows more effectively, the outcome of the battle might have ended otherwise. The cavalry would certainly have suffered higher losses. Through the centuries, several myths have sprung up around this battle. One such account even claimed that Matano's warriors first thought that mice had gnawed through the bowstrings.

TAK 1-10

TAK 1-11

photos TAK 1-10 & 1-11

Takeda Nobuyoshi's grave. The grave is located next to the Ganseiji Shrine, in Nirasaki city.

Due in part to this demonstration of his strategic skills, Nobuyoshi soon became a vital member of Yoritomo's military force. On the 18th or 20th of October (sources differ), only a couple of months after Nobuyoshi's triumph, a new battle took place near the Fuji River. Nobuyoshi defeated General Taira Koremori and his captains Taira Tadanori and Tadakiyo. The following day, Nobuyoshi was awarded the title of *Shugo* (Provincial constable; later, military governor) of Suruga.

THE POSTS OF SHUGO AND JITÔ

Shugo was a position that served as a representative of the central government. It was granted to families demonstrating great skill and ability in both military and civil matters. This position held little appeal, because there seem to be no substantial landholdings attached to the post. Because of this, when a person was promoted to *Shugo* of a province he might decide to remain where he was, or even set up an office in Kamakura, accepting the post as *Shugo* but not moving to the new province. In the case of the Takeda family, they apparently held the office of *Shugo* from 1180 to 1582. Judging by the length of time they administered the position they must have performed well; if not they would have surely been relieved from office. The *Shugo* was responsible for peace within the province and called on to organize troops to serve Kamakura during times of war. The *Shugo* also served Kamakura on all judicial matters in the province. The origin of this post can be traced back to 1180. It was in this year that Takeda Nobuyoshi was given the title of *Shugo* of Kai. After the Genpei War (1185) the Minamoto set up a military government in Kamakura (Southwest of Tokyo) and the *Shugo* system started to come into widespread practice.

Another post of great importance during the Kamakura period (1192-1333) was that of a *jitô* (a steward - the lord of a manor). A person was promoted to *jitô* over a village or several villages and his responsibilities were similar to those of a *Shugo*, but on a much smaller scale. The Kamakura government was responsible for promoting people into the position of a *jitô*. These people were usually, but not always, warriors. The *jitô* enjoyed extensive freedom and were exempt from interference, to a certain degree, from the *Shugo*. This freedom sometimes led to abuse of the post. Warriors proved to be the most abusive of the position.

photo TAK 1-12

From this point we can see across the area where Isawa Nobumitsu's mansion would have been located. Picture taken from the top of the castle-ruins of Kôfu castle.

KYÔTO AND KAMAKURA

By this time Kyôto had become the capital of Japan, and it was here that the Emperor and his Court lived and ruled. They had enjoyed dominance over the empire for eight centuries, but things were about to change. Prior to the Genpei

War of 1180-85 the Emperor ruled the land with the support of powerful families - some held rank with the Court, but others were pure samurai who had grown to be a problem for the Emperor. Over time, these samurai began to see themselves as the true power in Japan, not the Emperor. When Minamoto Yoritomo was given the order to subdue the Taira clan in 1180 he set up base in a town called Kamakura, to the southwest of modern day Tokyo. From here he led his campaigns against the Taira clan. The result was five years of bloody war throughout Japan. It culminated with the destruction of the Taira army at Dannoura in 1185. Minamoto Yoritomo came out as a battle-hardened warrior, hungry for more power. The Emperor and his Court realized the problems Yoritomo could create if they did not do what he wanted, and in 1192 they bestowed upon him the title of *Shôgun*.

The Minamoto family was then the true power in the empire, but however unimportant their voices had become the Emperor and his Court still had some say in how the government was run. Sadly though, the Minamoto rule as *Shôgun* was short lived. Another family had climbed up the ladder of power to challenge the Minamoto and the Emperor. The Hôjô clan had been watchful for an opportunity to claim more power during Yoritomo's reign. When Yoritomo died in 1199 his sons, Yoriie and Sanetomo, accepted the mantle of rulership, but were not cut from the same cloth as their father. Their inability to rule was something the Hôjô clan tried to exploit. Gradually, they schemed and manipulated their way to a position from which they could move against the Minamoto. When Sanetomo, the last Minamoto in the direct Yoritomo line, was assassinated in 1219 the Kamakura *Bakufu* (another term for *Shogunate*) was taken over by Hôjô Tokimasa. From 1219 to 1333 the Hôjô ruled Japan, not as *Shôgun*, but as the *Hôjô Shikken*. Their mismanagement of the land eventually brought about their collapse. In 1333 the Emperor Go-Daigo, along with many powerful warrior houses, defeated the Hôjô and the Kamakura government was no more.

llustration 1

The use of a *horo*. Depicted is a cavalryman wearing *O-yoroi* armor, riding for safety while the enemy shoots arrows at him. Because he uses a *horo*, the enemy does not have any real target to aim at. The *horo* was in use until the 16th century when it received a new role - as a heraldic device. Its origin is difficult to say, but it was in use before the Genpei Wars (1180-1185). It was made of a piece of silk cloth over a framework of bamboo or whale-beard. Not all *horo* had an inside framework, some simply hung down the back. It was only when the cavalryman was in motion that this type of horo looked like a balloon. The size of the *horo* varied dramatically, but it usually covered the wearer's back and head.

NOBUYOSHI'S DOWNFALL

The Genpei War ultimately became a tragedy for Takeda Nobuyoshi and his sons. During the early years of the war, Nobuyoshi was successful, too much so for his own good. The influence and military strength of the Takeda family made them a power to be reckoned with. As the war continued, Yoritomo gradually realized that the Takeda family might challenge his own position in the country. Both Nobuyoshi and one of his sons, Ichijô Tadayori, showed great promise in administration and politics, and this did not escape the notice of eyes in Kamakura, the unofficially established seat of the military government. Yoritomo decided that the Minamoto had become powerful and dangerous enough that drastic action was called for. In 1184, he invited Tadayori to Kamakura and had the Takeda general cut down before his very eyes. At the same time, Nobuyoshi was dismissed from his official position as *Shugo* of Suruga, effective immediately. With this violent, but unavoidable measure, Yoritomo felt that he had the Takeda family under control. Takeda Nobuyoshi became a stricken man, and retired from

photo TAK 1-13

The tomb of Minamato Yoritomo
(1147-1199). It is located in
Kamakura city, where he founded his
Shogunate in 1192.

public life. Plagued by poor health, the last years of his life were a sad chapter
in an otherwise exciting and colorful existence. Before his death in the Takeda
residence in 1186, he named his son, Nobumitsu, as his successor. At the time of
his father's death, Nobumitsu went by the name of Isawa Gorô Nobumitsu.

A new source indicates that a certain Takeda Ariyoshi was appointed heir, not Nobumitsu
as previously thought. He was an older brother to Nobumitsu and therefore the position was
rightfully his. According to this source Nobumitsu did not become the Takeda lord until
1200, when Ariyoshi died. At that point Isawa Gorô Nobumitsu supposedly took over the
Takeda family and changed his name to Takeda Nobumitsu. Very little information exists
on Takeda Ariyoshi, making this new information difficult to verify.

ISAWA NOBUMITSU

After his *genpuku* ceremony, Nobumitsu decided to move to the village of Isawa, where
he adopted the village name. Most samurai families were started in this way; sons of
noblemen settled in villages or districts where they built fortresses or castles to use as
administrative and military headquarters. Many took the name of the closest town or mountain
as their family name. Isawa continued, however, to regard himself as a member of the Takeda
family, and to supply them with military support when necessary.

Yoritomo still considered the Takeda family neutralized, but to make sure, he kept
Nobumitsu so busy that he would have little opportunity to plot revenge. He intended to
place Nobumitsu in the foremost ranks in any battle the Minamoto army might fight. In this

way, he would keep the Takeda family in line, while ensuring maximum performance from their cavalry through Nobumitsu's skills as a general in battle. In his handling of Nobumitsu, Yoritomo had to tread a fine line. If he pressed the Takeda too hard it might lead to revolution and treason, so Yoritomo always gave praise where praise was due, but never allowed Nobumitsu to wield as much power as Nobuyoshi had. Because of his position, Nobumitsu became one of the leading generals in the war with the Fujiwara family in the late 1180's. The Fujiwara had a powerful grip on the northern part of Honshû, resulting in a series of violent battles over the region. Although it was a difficult campaign, the conflict eventually ended with a complete victory for the Minamoto army.

The political pressure on Nobumitsu abated after Yoritomo's death in 1199. There are many indications that though Nobumitsu and Yoritomo were hardly the best of friends, they at least respected each other. Yoritomo took pains to treat Nobumitsu in the same manner as he did any other competent general; and Nobumitsu was duly rewarded after each successful campaign or battle. This was standard procedure throughout most of Japan's history. A reward might consist of a sword, an important administrative post or being named ruler of a province. At the time of Yoritomo's death, after years of constant war, Nobumitsu had become one of the mightiest generals in the Shogunate's military hierarchy. It might be said that Yoritomo knew how to reward a loyal servant, as long as he toed the line. One might speculate on Nobumitsu's response if he had not been treated fairly, but no evidence has ever been found to indicate that he plotted revenge for the treatment of his family.

Ch. 3 – Nobumitsu and the Jôkyû Rebellion

During the peaceful period that followed Yoritomo's death, Nobumitsu was able to turn his attention to family affairs and the administrative task of governing the province. This proved to be a short-lived homecoming. The Kamakura government needed his strategic skills; and in 1221 he and his cavalry were selected to help put down the *Jôkyû no ran* (Jôkyû Rebellion). This was a conflict between Emperor Go-Toba in Kyôto and the government in Kamakura, and is also referred to as the Jôkyû Period (1219-1221).

Go-Toba was anxious to restore the authority of the throne, and his primary objective was to overthrow the government in Kamakura. Kamakura heard rumors about the Emperor's ambitions for Kyôto, but chose to await developments. Go-Toba made repeated efforts to instigate an armed uprising, but his lack of allies initially forced him to be cautious. His contempt for the Kamakura regime would eventually lead to his downfall, driving him to commit to a course of action without adequate support from the other lords. The government in Kamakura was uncertain about how to react to the Emperor's impertinence. Some officials preferred a defensive strategy, while others called for military intervention. With considerable reluctance, a military response was chosen. A mobilization order was sent to the 15 provinces in the east. Soldiers from these provinces were organized into military units, and Kamakura chose generals to lead the campaign. Isawa Nobumitsu was chosen to lead the Tôsandô (Nakasendô) army, quite possibly because he had advocated military action at council meetings. The Kamakura coalition army consisted of Nobumitsu's army and two other divisions. Hôjô Yasutoki, who would advance along the Tôkaidô road, led the first of these divisions. Hôjô Tomotoki, who intended to follow the Hokurikudô road, led the second.

TOWARDS KYÔTO

Nobumitsu led his army out of Kamakura on May 25th, 1221. He departed Musashi and marched through Shinano Province. Many families in Shinano were willing to ally themselves with Nobumitsu. Among these was the Suwa family, which had mobilized its entire military force. On June 4th, the forces of Nobumitsu and Hôjô Yasutoki joined by the Kiso River, which formed a natural border between the Mino and Owari Provinces. When Nobumitsu's army crossed the Mino border, his forces, bolstered by Yasutoki's soldiers, numbered almost 50,000 men.

Go-Toba's spies kept him informed of his enemy's movements. He ordered his generals Fujiwara Hideyasu, Yamada Shigetada, and Miura Taneyoshi to counter the advance. With only 10,000 men, their prospects were poor, but they obeyed. According to some sources, they were outnumbered by as much as 10 to 1. The Emperor's troops left Kyôto on June 3rd. They made camp along the Kiso River with a single resolve: to prevent their adversaries from fording the river.

The Kamakura army split up into smaller divisions and attempted to cross the river at nine different points. The government troops pressed forward and slowly approached the opposite bank of the river. Arrows shot by the Kamakura army rained down by the hundreds, creating large breaches in the Emperor's defenses. The government cavalry exploited this situation and attacked the Emperor's foot soldiers. What was once a peaceful river had become a place of violence, and weapons were soon covered with blood. The battle raged until evening, when the numerically superior Kamakura army finally gained a foothold on the opposite bank. Once the Kamakura forces had crossed the river their cavalry obliterated the Emperor's camp. They were followed by foot soldiers that swept in and slaughtered the remnants of the Kyôto army desperately seeking shelter in the thick vegetation. Wounded soldiers were shown no mercy, and hundreds were decapitated. The Emperor's troops had no possibility of success; not only were they numerically inferior, but also the simple awareness of their slim chances undoubtedly weakened their fighting morale.

NOBUMITSU'S CAVALRY

Nobumitsu's cavalry formed the vanguard of the Kamakura attack, and performed with distinction, particularly when crossing the river. They pursued the enemy deep into Owari Province, thus preventing the organization of a new line of defense. A violent storm put an end to the pursuit, forcing the government troops to return to camp for a well-deserved rest. The downpour lasted several days, making battle extremely difficult, but Nobumitsu's Tôsandô army gradually neared Kyôto.

Despite the indisputable superiority of Nobumitsu's forces, Yamada Shigetada had managed to regroup the

remnants of the Kyôto army and formed a new line of defense along the Kuize River. Yamada's men fought courageously in this last stand, but without reinforcements they had no chance of success. This defense also failed and the Kyôto army was hounded from the battlefield.

Once again, weather influenced the battle. Rain poured down for five days, and the Uji River flooded, hindering further progress towards Kyôto. The water level reached record heights and the solitary bridge over the river was washed away, isolating the Kamakura army. They had no option but to wait for the water to recede and allow them to continue their march. On June 14th the government forces finally resumed their march towards Kyôto. Go-Toba's forces had used the intervening time to organize a new line of defense along the Uji River, but this also fell quickly, and the Kyôto army was once again chased from the battlefield. The Emperor's generals finally lost all hope of defending the capital. They were forced to admit that the battle was lost and flight was the only option. The Kamakura battalion continued to advance on Kyôto, and the last stragglers were hunted down near the city. On June 15th, 1221, Hôjô Yasutoki rode into Kyôto with his army, and the Jôkyû Rebellion died.

Isawa Nobumitsu was rewarded with the title *Shugo* of Aki for his military success; and evidence implies that he also kept his other title as *Shugo* of Kai. The new title and office would strongly influence the future of the Takeda family. After the war, Isawa Nobumitsu left Kamakura and moved 800 kilometers to Aki province in the west. The *fudai* families Akiyama, Naitô and Saegusa followed. In all more than 2,000 vassals followed Nobumitsu to Aki. The history of Kai during the next century is a mystery because of the scarcity of historical references, perhaps due to this migration.

TWO PROVINCES

Nobumitsu left Kai in the hands of reliable subjects who administered the province in his absence. The Aki branch of the Takeda family (also known as the Wakasa Takeda family) had its period of greatness in the fifteenth and early sixteenth century.

Despite the distance between the two provinces, Nobumitsu governed both Aki and Kai wisely. Kai had been a focal point of trade and agriculture for centuries. Takeda Manor near Isawa Village developed into an important trade center. A market was held on the fourth of each month, and peasants and artisans brought produce and wares to the manor, where they were sold to travelling merchants. Horse breeding remained important in Kai; the sale of horses was extremely profitable, and presumably provided Nobumitsu with considerable income. The flourishing commercial activity helped strengthen his administrative apparatus and subsidize the powerful Takeda war machine.

Although Nobumitsu had entrusted the administration of the Kai province to *loyal* officials, he inspected the province whenever he passed through on the way to Kamakura. This gave him an opportunity to ensure that everything was in order and that his subordinates were carrying out his policies. Although punishment for corruption and crime were severe, the distances lords had to travel to inspect their lands ensured that disloyal officers were common. Nobumitsu was often in Kamakura while in the service of the *Bakufu* government, and commuting from Aki must have been time-consuming. Both provinces apparently flourished under his reign, which seems to have been a good period for both himself and his family. His third son, Nobumasa, assumed leadership of the clan upon Nobumitsu's death in 1248. The reason why his first-born son, Tomonobu, didn't take over the family might be due to the fact that he left for Kurosaka in Yatsushiro district to start his own family. There he built a manor, and changed his name to Kurosaka Tomonobu. Next in line was the second son, Nobutada, but he had brought shame upon himself in a military campaign in Shinano in 1241, and was subsequently cut from the will, becoming an outcast. This opened the way for Nobumasa, and surpassing the achievements of Nobumitsu was a challenge that Nobumasa took seriously.

Illustration 2

The use of *kanasaibô* (also known as *kanabô*). This fearsome weapon rose in popularity during the 14th century. Here the user strikes at an enemy's head. The weapon's use declined during the 16th century when new weapons, like the matchlock gun, were introduced. The *kanasaibô* could vary between 2 and 3.6 meters in length. It weighed between 3 kg and 6 kg. The most popular materials used in its construction were oak, yew or box tree wood. About two thirds of the club was covered with iron strips or plates, covered with spikes.

CULTURE IN KAI

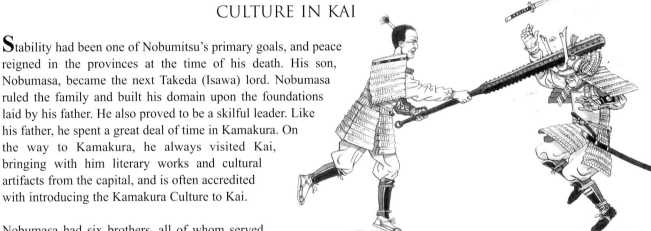

Stability had been one of Nobumitsu's primary goals, and peace reigned in the provinces at the time of his death. His son, Nobumasa, became the next Takeda (Isawa) lord. Nobumasa ruled the family and built his domain upon the foundations laid by his father. He also proved to be a skilful leader. Like his father, he spent a great deal of time in Kamakura. On the way to Kamakura, he always visited Kai, bringing with him literary works and cultural artifacts from the capital, and is often accredited with introducing the Kamakura Culture to Kai.

Nobumasa had six brothers, all of whom served under the *Bakufu* government in Kamakura. Their duties ranged from quelling rebellions to protecting government representatives visiting Kyôto on official business. The Takeda (Isawa) family had close contact with the Kamakura regime during these years, and the government reciprocated their loyalty. Ambitious neighbors avoided conflicts with the two provinces, since a war with the Takeda clan would have inevitably led to a war with the government in Kamakura. The brothers, however, did not spend all their time in Kamakura. Nobumasa also assigned them duties in Kai such as the construction and restoration of temples, the planting of rice fields, and the production of local goods. It is clear that Nobumasa governed Kai efficiently. Regardless of whether he was in Aki or Kamakura, he made certain that competent officials carried out his orders. Both Kai and Aki were prosperous provinces when he died in 1265.

photo TAK 1-14

A fence around a military camp, castle or fortress, or even used on the battlefield itelf. Behind this obstacle rows of archers or *teppô* soldiers (after 1543) could fire on the enemy lines. The fence was made from wood or bamboo.

Upon Nobumasa's death, his eldest son, Nobutoki, became heir. He was undoubtedly apprehensive about governing such widely separated provinces, but presumably found encouragement in the successful administrations of his father and grandfather. Like his father, he employed his younger brothers - Masatsuna, Nobushige, Masanaga, Nobuyasu, and Nobutsuna - to help govern the two provinces. They served in Kai, Aki and Kamakura. All of them were skilled in horse riding and the martial arts, and were certainly regarded as loyal and honest samurai by the government in Kamakura.

Historical documents from this period are scarce and those that have survived are vague. There are indications that Nobutoki efficiently carried out his duties as head of the family. Sources claim that he died early, and that others, including his younger brother Masatsuna, actually governed during much of Nobutoki's lifetime. Other evidence suggests that Nobutoki governed for a long period of time and was not replaced by Masatsuna. Regardless of who governed during Nobutoki's lifetime his son, Tokitsuna, apparently inherited his father's title, and became head of the family. We know little about the life of Tokitsuna. One source reports that he fought his first battle, along with his father, in 1274.

Information about the third Takeda lord, Tokitsuna's son Nobumune, is so sparse that almost nothing is known about his life. One source credits him with the construction of Kanayama Castle in Aki. This was a *yamashiro* (mountain castle). During this era, it was common to build auxiliary fortifications in addition to the main fortifications. These were often constructed near strategic access roads. Kanayama Castle's secondary fortresses were Koi, Fuchû, Takamatsu, Mibu, Tomo and Kunishige. The Aki Takeda clan used Kanayama Castle as their main headquarters until 1541, when it was stormed by the Ôuchi family.

Ch. 4 – The Nanbokuchô Period

THE NANBOKUCHÔ WAR

Nobumune died in 1330 and his son, Nobutake, became the head of the Aki Takeda clan. He led the family during the Nanbokuchô period, which was characterized by 50 years of almost continuous warfare. This was one of the most turbulent intervals in Japanese history.

The origins of the Nanbokuchô War can be traced to the latter part of the thirteenth century, when two separate imperial families developed. These were the Go-Fukakusa (senior) and the Kameyama (junior) families. Succession to the throne normally alternated between these two clans. Though the political situation was unstable before 1318, this arrangement had functioned earlier without serious complications. However, when Go-Daigo (1288-1339) was chosen as Emperor, the situation became more complex. The preceding emperors had been children when they were nominated, and after a few years on the throne they had more-or-less voluntarily abdicated in response to pressures from Kamakura, as it was easier to control a child on the throne than an adult emperor. Go-Daigo, however, was in his thirties when he became Emperor, and had no intention of being manipulated or forced to abdicate. The Hôjô government in Kamakura played along with him for a while, but when they realized that he had no plan to follow their 'suggestions' on how to rule, the truce collapsed. Even worse, in 1326 Go-Daigo named his own son as heir to the throne, ignoring Kamakura's 'recommendations' regarding an heir. The Hôjô government realized that drastic action would be necessary.

Go-Daigo spent much of his time seeking support for an armed uprising against Kamakura, and he received encouragement from various parts of the country. Dissatisfaction with the Kamakura government was widespread, and many lords were willing to support him. Unfortunately for Go-Daigo, the most powerful families remained faithful to Kamakura.

The reason Go-Daigo worked to overthrow the Hôjô was that he wanted the seat of power back in the Imperial House. His efforts did not go as planned, however, and a new warrior family, the Ashikaga, seized power after the Hôjô clan's destruction. From 1338 to 1573 the Ashikaga were the ruling family of Japan. Even though their power began to decline after the outbreak of the Ônin War in 1467 they held the office of *Shôgun* until 1573. They claimed the Muromachi area in Kyôto as their own, placing a deputy under the *Shôgun* in

Kamakura to manage the government and keep an eye on the eastern provinces. The long distances combined with the diverse personalities in power became a source of constant difficulty. Time and time again there would be problems between the Kamakura office and the government in Kyôto, and several military conflicts occurred between the two entities during the 15th century.

One of Go-Daigo's collaborators revealed his plans to the Kamakura regime, and the Hôjô clan deployed a punitive expedition of about 3,000 men against Kyôto, led by General Nikaidô. Their purpose was to arrest those implicated in the plot to overthrow the Kamakura government, and force the Emperor to realize that the Kamakura government would ultimately determine who would be emperor. General Nikaidô executed at least ten of the conspirators, and Go-Daigo yielded to the government council, if only temporarily.

When Go-Daigo learned of the government's plan to replace him with one of the Go-Fukakusa line, he decided to move his court away from Kyôto and beyond the influence of the Rokuhara army, the Kamakura government's stationary force in Kyôto. He traveled to the Tôdaiji and Tônanji temples at Nara, where he was joined by General Asuke Shigenori and 500 *Sôhei* (warrior-monks). Go-Daigo's small force entrenched itself in a fortress atop Mount Kasagi. This fortress was actually a cluster of temples. It was then that the Kamakura regime realized that a military campaign against the Emperor was inevitable and dispatched a 20,000-man strong government army to defeat the rebellious emperor. One of the generals in the Rokuhara army was Takeda Nobutake and his legendary cavalry. Another participant was Isawa Masayoshi, a clan chieftain from Kai.

The battle began on September 6th, 1331, when the Rokuhara army deployed around Mount Kasagi. Once the fortress was completely surrounded, the troops were ordered to begin a siege. The fortress was difficult to capture, because the warrior-monks were well prepared, and had reinforced the entire fortress. Climbing the mountain also proved difficult, and a massive, coordinated attack would have taken so long that the losses would have been unjustifiable. The fortress's natural defensive position enabled the 500 brave *sôhei* to hold the enemy at bay for twenty days. They were finally forced to surrender on September 28th, after battle fatigue and hunger had taken their toll.

Go-Daigo had no intention of being taken prisoner. The evening before the fortress fell he escaped into the night under cover of torrential rain. He managed to sneak through enemy lines, but was eventually captured and returned to Kyôto on October 1st. He was still legally the Emperor, but the Council had to prevent him from promoting further unrest. Too popular to execute, he was banished to the island of Oki, where he would no longer pose a threat to the Kamakura regime.

AGAINST KUSUNOKI MASASHIGE

After Go-Daigo had been arrested and escorted back to Kyôto, the Kamakura (Rokuhara) Army was ordered to attack Akasaka, a *yamashiro* situated in Kawachi province. Kusunoki Masashige, a staunch supporter of the emperor, was forced to defend himself against the 20,000-man strong Kamakura Army with somewhere between 500 and a 1,000 men. Nobutake's cavalry was also involved in the onslaught and prepared to attack the castle from behind. The blast of a *horagai* (conch-shell

Illustration 3

A female samurai, around 1181. Tomoe Gozen wears *O-yoroi* armor; she was the favorite mistress of the famous general Kiso Yoshinaka. It is identical to armor used by male samurai. The *naginata* weapon she wields was a favorite weapon among women and warrior monks (*sôhei*).

trumpet) on the 17th of October 1331 heralded the attack. This was answered with a barrage of arrows from the ramparts, slowing the charge.

Masashige had planned his defense well. He poured boiling water on his adversaries and rolled logs down the mountainside, bowling over entire ranks of men. Dead and wounded were soon strewn across the mountainside, hindering the attack. After five days of savage battle, the Kamakura Army finally reached the outer walls of the castle. Masashige's exhausted men were gradually driven into the inner fortress. Although the defenders of the castle fought valiantly, they were finally overrun. Torching the castle to camouflage his escape, Masashige climbed over the wall and disappeared into the surrounding vegetation. Nobutake and his allies searched for Masashige in vain - he had vanished without a trace. After the battle, Nobutake and his troops returned home, reaching Kanayama Castle in Aki on November 1st.

In Aki, Nobutake closely followed the activities of the Go-Daigo sympathizers within his own and nearby provinces. These sympathizers supported the Court in the south, and would rebel if an opportunity presented itself.

Takeda Nobutake enjoyed a year of peace before once again going into battle. His adversary was again Kusunoki Masashige, who now commanded 1,000 men. Reports reached Nobutake that Masashige's soldiers had sought refuge in Chihaya Castle, near the village of Akasaka at the foot of Mount Kongô. Chihaya Castle was situated between two rivers, which served as natural barriers to attack. This castle would prove a formidable challenge to the Kamakura Army. Again, Nobutake's cavalry attacked the castle from the rear, where they could not be observed. From this angle the mountainside was also steep and inaccessible. The attack was met with tactics similar to those with which Masashige had defended Akasaka Castle. The soldiers were met with a rain of arrows, a hail of stones and boulders; and as before, rolling logs and boiling water. Kusunoki Masashige ignored the martial code of honor, using any tactic that he considered effective - even pouring excrement on the enemy.

Masashige was well prepared, and had stored large quantities of water, food and supplies in preparation for the siege. Although the Kamakura Army cut off the food and water supply, the besieged castle still managed to hold out for more than one hundred days. Finally, the Kamakura Army launched a massive attack on February 1st 1333, and succeeded in capturing the outer defenses of the castle. Swords, spears and *naginata* (halberds) glinted in the sun. The battlefield was strewn with the bodies of the besiegers and besieged. After several hours of furious battle, one of the Masashige's captains, Hirano Shôgen, realized that the battle was lost, and surrendered with 280 men. Once again, Masashige managed to escape. Although the Kamakura Army searched diligently, Masashige disappeared as if swallowed by the earth.

Illustration 4

Six severed heads on display. After the head viewing ceremony the heads where hung upon a rack such as this for public display. The small labels attached to the ears or to the topknots inform people of who was killed and by whom - of course the enemy's name was occasionally unknown, but who killed him was important when a reward was at stake.

THE RETURN OF GO--DAIGO

Major political changes had taken place while the battle was raging at Chihaya Castle. Several powerful clans, resenting the Hôjô Regency in Kamakura, had joined the Go-Daigo faction, wreaking political chaos. Takeda Nobutake was in a very difficult situation, largely because he was married to the niece of Ashikaga Takauji, who had publicly declared his support for Go-Daigo. Because of these familial ties Nobutake might have felt obligated to follow Takauji's lead and join the rebels. Instead, he decided to procrastinate before taking sides. He feigned illness, ordered his soldiers to pack for the journey, and set off towards home. They went first to Kai, but some evidence suggests that they also continued on to Aki.

The exiled emperor, Go-Daigo, had spent most of his time on the island of Oki planning his flight. In the spring of 1333, after nearly two years in exile, he finally managed to escape from the island. He fled to the provinces west of Kyôto, where he had trustworthy allies. Go-Daigo proposed that they should muster an army, recapture the imperial city of Kyôto, and restore to the throne its former power and prestige. His proposal was accepted and the lords summoned soldiers to carry out the Emperor's campaign. Once the army had gathered, Go-Daigo marched on Kyôto. On the 7th of May, Ashikaga Takauji's forces attacked the Rokuhara troops stationed in Kyôto. The city was taken with little resistance from the enemy.

TAK 1-15

TAK 1-16

photo TAK 1-15 & 1-16

The city of Kamakura. For a period of nearly 150 years (1185-1333) this was the administrative capital of Japan.

On the 8th of May, Lord Nitta Yoshisada, who had supported the government previously, saw which way the tide was turning and declared war on Kamakura, allying himself with Go-Daigo. Nobutake received a letter (the author is unknown, but quite possibly from Takauji himself) on May 10th encouraging him to join Go-Daigo's forces. Perhaps Go-Daigo succeeded because several powerful clans had turned against Kamakura, providing troops and able strategists such as Ashikaga Takauji and Nitta Yoshisada. Strategic and tactical skills were vital to success during the period.

A great deal took place during very few days, and on May 18th Nitta Yoshisada's army of 20,000 men stormed Kamakura. For several days, Yoshisada's army fought against the Hôjô clan's soldiers in and around the town of Kamakura. The regent (*Shikken*) for the *Shôgun* in Kamakura at this time was Hôjô Takatoki. The position of *Shikken* (a position below the *Shôgun*) was established in 1203, and from its inception the position had been

A MOUNTED TAKEDA

A Takeda cavalryman ready for war. Before the *Sengoku Jidai* (1467-1615) it was the samurai on horseback that made the difference in battle. Skilled in the use of bow and arrow, sword and spear, he was a fighting artist, certainly a samurai to be fighting with, not against. As was proven many times, mounted samurai were often the difference between victory and defeat on the battlefield. They could make lightning swift attacks into enemy lines, maneuver quickly across large amounts of terrain, and even provide a good deal of missile fire when required.

THE GENPEI WAR (1180)

In this scene the Takeda cavalry is attacking the enemy camp of Matano and Tachibana early in the morning. Unable to don their armor quickly, and with headaches after the previous night's sake party, the soldiers were unable to defend themselves effectively. Even their archers were caught unaware when they discovered that Takeda forces had cut many of the army's bowstrings during the night. This battle was an easy victory for the well-prepared Takeda force, and those soldiers that attempted to escape the battle were mercilessly cut down. In the background, one of the cavalry soldiers carries a small horo on his back – the horo served as a protective device, deflecting arrows and smaller stones.

THE JŌKYŪ REBELLION (1221)

Legend has it that Isawa Nobumitsu was the first across the Kiso River. As the Kamakura army struggles to hold the enemy at bay. The fighting lasted for many hours, but in the end the Kamakura army was unstoppable. The strategy that the Kamakura army used was simple: ford the river along several points at once making it impossible for the enemy to concentrate their forces in one place. Both sides used hundreds of foot soldiers with bows (note the pavises used by the archers), but in the end it was the cavalry that broke through and won the day.

TAKEDA ON THE MARCH (1240)

Here the illustrator depicts what the Takeda on route to war or Kamakura would look like. The *ashigaru* in the foreground carries the *hata-jirushi* flag with the Takeda family crest (*kamon*). Next rides a cavalry soldier with a small *horo* on his back. Behind the cavalryman march the porters, boxed supplies on their back. When the need arose, even these men were expected to fight. In the background a line of Takeda soldiers can be seen. These are mostly *ashigaru*, carrying *naginata*. *Ashigaru* made up the bulk of many Japanese armies. They were not as well trained or armed as samurai, but the need for numbers on the battlefield ensured that these soldiers were always at hand.

AN EXECUTION (1330)

This scene shows two conspirators just before their beheadings along a riverbank. The attendants prepare the prisoners for their last moments by tilting the heads of their victims slightly forward. Clearly seen is their hairstyle, typical prior to the 1400's. With his back to us the commander supervises the entire ritual. Some warriors were denied the right to commit seppuku, or refused the face-saving path of suicide. These prisoners were probably not important enough to be offered the path of suicide, and for expedience sake are simply to be killed.

THE ATTACK ON CHIHAYA (1332)

This illustration shows how the attack on Chihaya fortress in 1332 might have looked. The 20,000-man strong Kamakura army besieged the fortress for a hundred day period, but in the end the defenders were forced to give up. The Takeda army under the command of Takeda Nobutake took part in this attack. In the foreground can be seen a warrior blowing on his *horagai*, giving the sound to attack. Next to him is a commander rallying his men forward. Rushing to attack, several of the samurai carry crude wooden shields to protect themselves from the defenders' arrows. These shields may have served as some protection against the missile fire, but would not have provided much defense against boiling oil or water spilled over the walls.

HUNTING FOR ENEMIES (1336)

Soldiers belonging to Ashikaga Takauji are hunting soldiers still loyal to the Emperor. The helmetless samurai in the upper right corner is welding a *kanasaibō* (club). An uncommon weapon, the *kanasaibō* was wooden with strips of metal running its length and could kill or cripple an enemy with a single blow when wielded with skill. The club became very popular during the Nanbokuchō period, and held this popularity towards the end of the 15th century when it was considered an obsolete weapon. The head served as crucial proof when claiming a reward. The cavalry commander supervises the search, but is ready for action, his sword unsheathed. The soldier carrying the spear has an antique sword – a straight *tachi* sword – attached to his belt. The first swords made or imported to Japan were shaped like this; the same sword type was used in China and Korea, and many were imported from these countries.

MOUNTAIN FORTRESS (1000-1500)

This is a typical mountain fortress from the year 1000 to the 1500's. This type of fortress could be seen on thousands of mountains throughout Japan, and usually consisted of a main compound (honmaru), and a second, sometimes third, compound. Although this is a typical layout for a mountain fortress, no two were built exactly alike. The same can be said of the field fortresses during that time. Among these fortresses were also larger ones that served as the main castle of a Lord. During the 1500's samurai added more and more stone to their fortifications. Towers were usually positioned at strategic points inside the fortress as well as atop important peaks nearby. Here we see a typical watchtower situated on a nearby peak. One of the soldiers stands watch while the other takes a brief break below. The inaccessibility of the fortress walls makes it easy to see why so many assaults ended in sieges.

THE THIRD ATTACK (1426)

Isshiki Mochiie had been ordered to deal with the Takeda, but against the inspiring leadership of Takeda Nobunaga Mochiie would face a total defeat. Isshiki had chosen the shortest route to Kai, but not the easiest. Nobunaga used his extensive knowledge of the terrain to his advantage. After the enemy had entered the trap the signal was sounded, and his men hurled stones and fired arrows at Isshiki's soldiers marching below. For Ashikaga in Kamakura it was all he could stand. After this humiliating defeat he took direct command of the next expedition against Nobunaga. The soldiers' armor had also changed quite a bit, with few O-yoroi seen in the field by this time.

BATTLE IN SHINANO (1466)

In March of 1466 Takeda Nobumasa, following orders, ventured into Shinano and marched straight into an enemy ambush. Already deep and still falling, the snow hindered both forces as they faced one another on the plane below Nobeyama Mountain. In this scene we see a hardened warrior monk (*sōhei*), armed with *naginata*, preparing to battle a charging samurai, while a nearby cavalry archer prepares to fire across the battlefield. *Haidate* (thigh-guards) had come into use by this time, but both the monk and the cavalryman still have metal-plates sewn directly onto their trousers. Nobumasa's and Shigeuji's men fought a bloody engagement on this battlefield, and when he returned the next day Nobumasa discovered that the lifeblood of over 500 men had mingled with the snow during the fight.

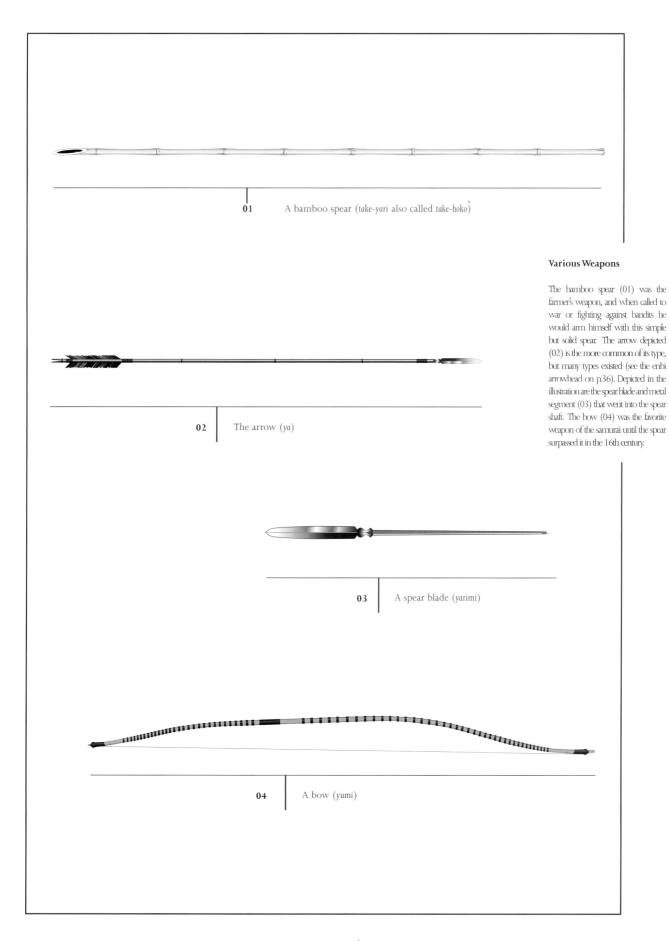

01   A bamboo spear (*take-yari* also called *take-hoko*)*

Various Weapons

The bamboo spear (01) was the farmer's weapon, and when called to war or fighting against bandits he would arm himself with this simple but solid spear. The arrow depicted (02) is the more common of its type, but many types existed (see the enbi arrowhead on p.36). Depicted in the illustration are the spear blade and metal segment (03) that went into the spear shaft. The bow (04) was the favorite weapon of the samurai until the spear surpassed it in the 16th century.

02 | The arrow (*ya*)

03   A spear blade (*yarimi*)

04   A bow (*yumi*)

Various Weapons

The *nagamaki* (06) was simply a spear shaft topped with a sword blade. It and the *naginata*, commonly referred to as a glaive (05), were fearsome weapons. These weapons were popular among female samurai and warrior-monks. The *enbi* arrowhead (07) was used to knock away portions of an enemy's armor. It required considerable skill with a bow to be used effectively.

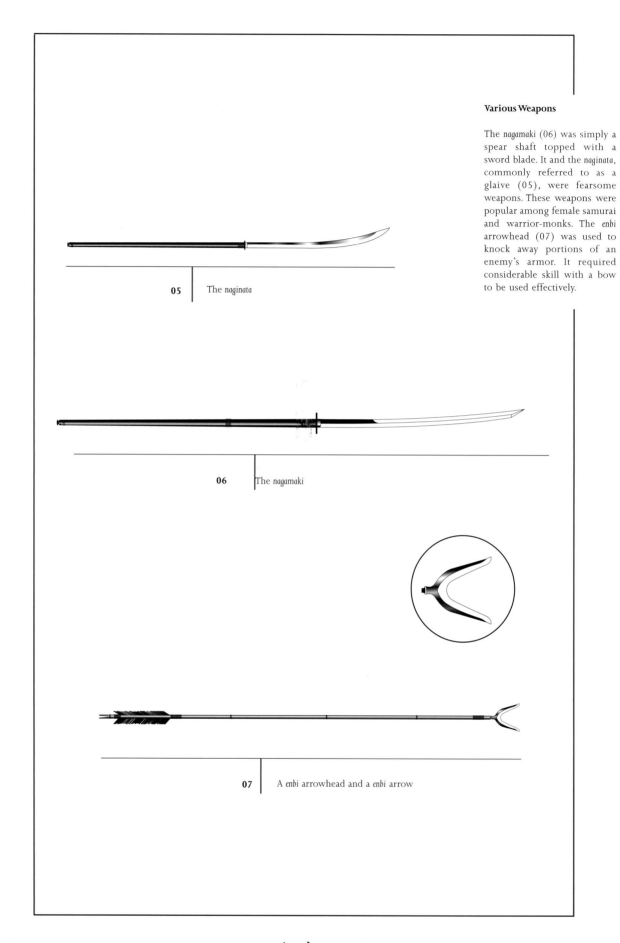

| 05 | The *naginata* |

| 06 | The *nagamaki* |

| 07 | A *enbi* arrowhead and a *enbi* arrow |

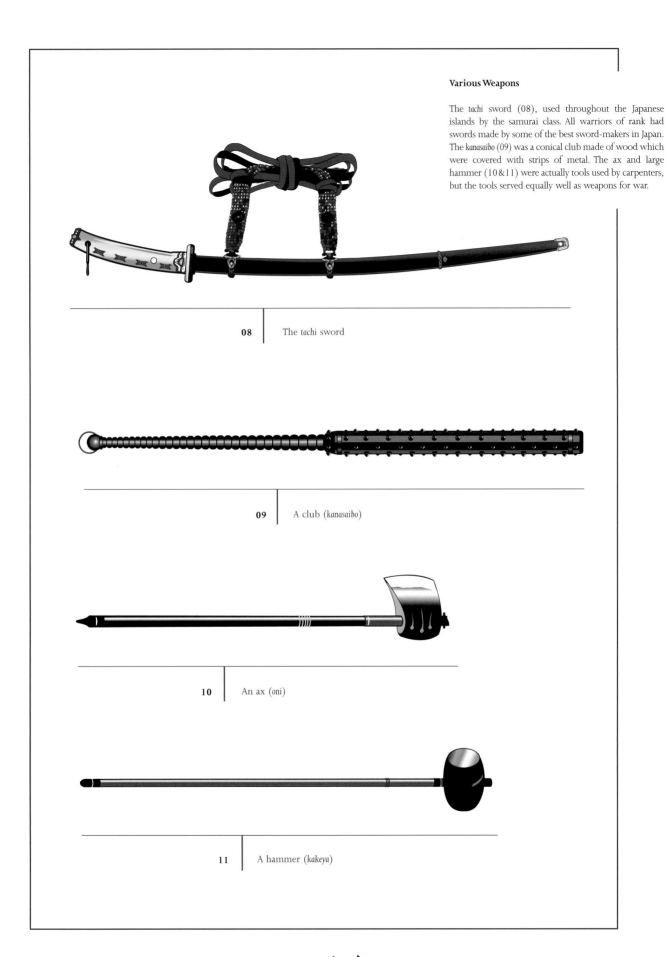

Various Weapons

The *tachi* sword (08), used throughout the Japanese islands by the samurai class. All warriors of rank had swords made by some of the best sword-makers in Japan. The *kanasaibo* (09) was a conical club made of wood which were covered with strips of metal. The ax and large hammer (10 & 11) were actually tools used by carpenters, but the tools served equally well as weapons for war.

| **08** | The *tachi* sword |

| **09** | A club (*kanasaibo*) |

| **10** | An ax (*oni*) |

| **11** | A hammer (*kakeya*) |

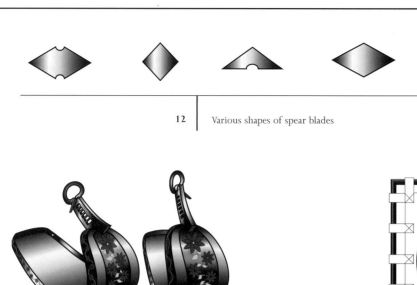

| 12 | Various shapes of spear blades

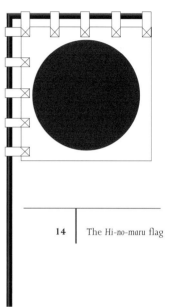

| 14 | The Hi-no-maru flag

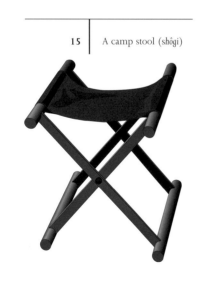

| 13 | Stirrups (*abumi*)

Various Equipment and Weapons

At top (12) we see the five most common spear blades used. The *abumi*, or stirrups (13), used in Japan were quite than those used by the Europeans. These stirrups were almost always made from iron and a swift kkick to the head from a rider could kill an opponent on foot. The *Hi-Ikki* forces that served the Takeda clan used the red sun disk flag. The Takeda clan had a similar flag from 1056 (14), but that flag was too precious to be carried into battle. The *shôgi* (15) was the commander's stool (often referred to as a campstool). Whenever a lord was away from his castle on campaign, a page would follow behind, carrying one of these stools. Civilians and warriors alike wore *Waraji* (16). A soldier could be expected to wear out several pairs while away on weeks long campaigns. .

| 15 | A camp stool (*shôgi*)

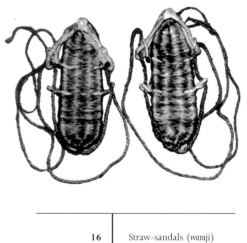

| 16 | Straw-sandals (*waraji*)

SEA OF JAPAN

PACIFIC OCEAN

HONSHÛ

SHIKOKU

KYÛSHÛ

DEWA
MUTSU
Sendai
SADO
ECHIGO
NOTO
ETCHÛ
SHIMOTSUKE
KÔSUKE
HITACHI
KAGA
HIDA
SHINANO
MUSASHI
SHIMOSA
ECHIZEN
MINO
KAI
Edo (TOKYO)
KASZUSA
WAKASA
Nakasendô
ÔMI
SAGAMI
Kamakura
AWA
TANGO
TANBA
MIKAWA
SURUGA
IZU
TÔTÔMI
OKI
TAJIMA
INABA
HÔKI
YAMASHIRO
Kyoto
Nagashima
HARIMA
SETTSU
IGA
ISE
MIMASAKA
BIZEN
IZUMI
SHIMA
IZUMO
BITCHÛ
IWAMI
BINGO
AWAJI
YAMATO
OWARI province
AKI
SANUKI
KAWACHI
TSUSHIMA
SUÔ
AWA
KII
NAGATO
Ôsaka
IKI
IYO
TOSA
CHIKUZEN
BUZEN
HIZEN
CHIKUGO
BUNGO
GOTÔ
ISLANDS
HIGO
HYÛGA
SATSUMA
ÔSUMI
TANEGASHIMA
YAKUSHIMA

—— Main roads

MAP 1

Map of Japan – 16th century
On this map are three of the four main islands of Japan, and their provinces. Hightlighted in dark green is the province of Kai, where Takeda clan ruled.

MAP 2

The Province of Kai
Kai povince and the border-provinces in the south and southeast. As we can see on this map the huge Mount Fuji is shared by Kai and Suruga Province, and for the people in both of these provinces the mountain was sacred.

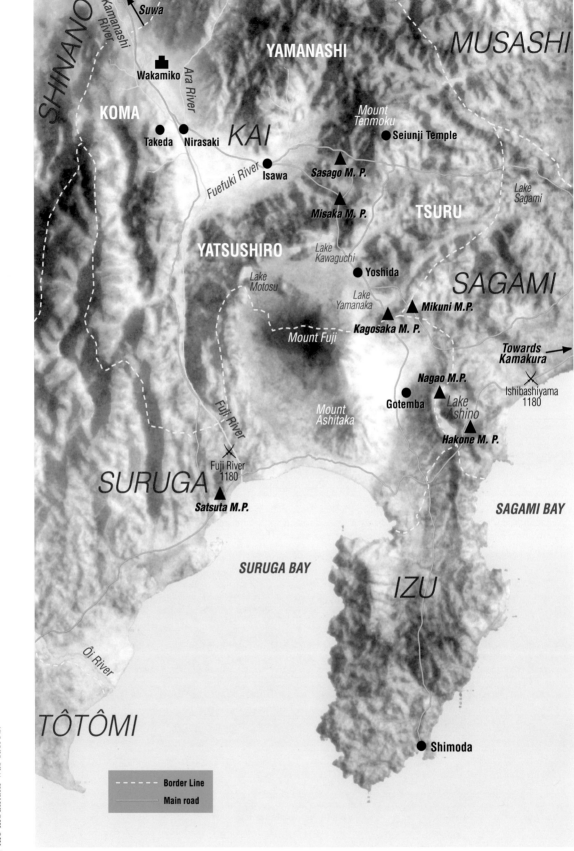

SHINANO

Kamanashi River

Suwa

Wakamiko

KOMA

Takeda Nirasaki

Ara River

KAI

Fuefuki River Isawa

YAMANASHI

MUSASHI

Mount Tenmoku

Seiunji Temple

▲ *Sasago M. P.*

▲ *Misaka M. P.*

TSURU

Lake Sagami

YATSUSHIRO

Lake Kawaguchi

Lake Motosu

● Yoshida

SAGAMI

Lake Yamanaka

▲ *Mikuni M.P.*

▲ *Kagosaka M. P.*

Mount Fuji

Nagao M.P.

▲

Gotemba ● *Lake Ashino*

Towards Kamakura

✕ Ishibashiyama 1180

Mount Ashitaka

▲ *Hakone M. P.*

Fuji River

SURUGA

✕ Fuji River 1180

▲ *Satsuta M.P.*

SAGAMI BAY

IZU

SURUGA BAY

Ôi River

TÔTÔMI

Shimoda ●

- - - - Border Line
──── Main road

photo TAK 1-17

A typical watch-fire. Used throughout Japan in camps, fortressesand castles. It was a metal basket with legs made from either wood, bamboo or metal.

photo TAK 1-18

A representative fireplace inside a samurai house. The size of these fireplaces varied, but the use of a square hole filled with sand was typical. This photo is taken inside the kuri building at Unpôji temple in Enzan city.

TAK 1-17

hereditary, always held by members of the Hôjô clan. Although Hôjô Takatoki defended himself well, the enemy's superior army was much too strong for the Kamakura samurai. Upon his defeat, Takatoki and his family committed *seppuku* (ritual suicide). Many other members of the Hôjô clan and their vassals also followed suit, joining their lord in death, preferring to die honorably rather than be captured. The battle for Kamakura was over by the 22nd of May. In early June Nitta Yoshisada led his army out of Kamakura, bound for Kyôto.

ASHIKAGA TAKAUJI'S REBELLION

Go-Daigo entered Kyôto in the beginning of June 1333. In keeping with his plan to reinstate the Imperial government, he immediately began to appoint loyal court members to important posts throughout the country. He also intended to curb the influence and power of the samurai class. Although Go-Daigo treated his victorious generals, Ashikaga Takauji and Nitta Yoshisada, with great respect, and praised them for their efforts, he had no intention in giving them more political power than they already possessed. The failure of the Emperor to reward his generals adequately would cost him dearly. By 1335 the relationship between Go-Daigo and Ashikaga Takauji began to deteriorate seriously. Without the consent of the Emperor, Takauji and his troops left Kyôto to quell a rebellion in Kamakura led by sympathizers of the Hôjô clan. Takeda Nobutake and his famous cavalry joined him. Not surprisingly, Takauji's forces crushed the rebellion in Kamakura easily.

Takauji built a new headquarters in the city, assumed the role of *Shôgun* in Kamakura, and showed no intention of returning to Kyôto. The Emperor sent several dispatches to Kamakura attempting to recall Takauji, without success. It appears that Takauji had already laid ambitious plans before his march on Kamakura. His actions naturally disturbed Go-Daigo, who probably suspected his motives. Takauji revealed his true intentions when he marched against Kyôto with his army in 1336. Go-Daigo's other great general, Nitta Yoshisada, had lost a large battle against Takauji at Takenoshita in December of the previous year and had adopted a wait-and-see attitude. Regardless of his intentions, Yoshisada was not at Kyôto to defend the Emperor and Go-Daigo, fearing for his life, fled the capital.

TAK 1-18

TAKEDA NOBUTAKE, SHUGO OF KAI

The Nanbokuchô War, a conflict between the two Imperial houses and the Ashikaga clan, lasted sixty years. Kai province was deeply involved in this struggle. Isawa Masayoshi, one of the Lords in Kai, had sided with the Emperor through years of war. Consequently, Ashikaga removed him from his position as *Shugo* of Kai. The office was awarded to one of Ashikaga's supporters, Takeda Nobutake. After slightly more than a century of absence, the Takeda clan was once again powerful in Kai. Historical evidence suggests that the Kai Takeda clan governed Kai for a greater part of this period. Takeda Nobutake served under Ashikaga Takauji until the death of the latter in 1358. Nobutake repeatedly distinguished himself in decisive battles, and became one of Ashikaga Takauji's most loyal and skilled generals. The day after Takauji's death, Nobutake shaved his head, became a priest, and withdrew from the public arena. He apparently did not thrive in his new life as a priest since he died about a year later, but his legend lived on. Takeda Nobutake's heroic deeds on the battlefield were well known throughout Japan. At the time of his death, his name was as familiar as other Japanese heroes, such as Ashikaga Takauji, Kusunoki Masashige and Nitta Yoshisada.

Ch. 5 – More Troubles for the Takeda

TAKEDA NOBUSHIGE

Takeda Nobutake's heir was his son Nobushige (in some literature the name is read as Nobunari). Nobushige inherited the property, goods, and land of his father, as well as the title of *Shugo* of Kai. It is at this time that Kai and Aki acquired separate *Shugos* (protectors). Nobushige's brother, Ujinobu, assumed the title of *Shugo* of Aki in 1358 when their father, Nobutake, chose to become a priest. (Some historians speculate that Nobushige and Ujinobu were one and the same). After this, each branch of the Takeda clan ruled its own province. The great physical distance between the two provinces also discouraged communication. A third prominent line of Takeda, the Wakasa Takeda clan, would descend from the Aki Takeda clan. This offshoot of the family, as well as the Aki and Kai branches, was destined to become involved in the turbulence of the sixteenth century.

According to sources, Nobushige engaged in numerous campaigns during the Nanbokuchô War (1336-1392), probably serving as an officer leading his own unit of cavalry. Nobushige retained the title of Lord of Aki throughout his lifetime. The title was often used as part of the name, e.g. *Takeda Aki no Kami*. Since only surnames and titles were used in contemporary sources, the actual names of individuals are often difficult to determine. During his lifetime, Nobushige built several temples and was involved in the restoration of several others. Unfortunately, due to meager source material, we know very little about Nobushige, except that he died in 1394 and his son, Nobuharu, became the new clan leader.

TAKEDA NOBUHARU

We do not know when Nobuharu was born, but it must have been near the middle of the 14th century. According to the source *Taheiki*, Nobuharu and his father took part in the campaign of 1352 under Ashikaga Takauji's flag. He is again mentioned in 1355, when he participated in the battle at Mount Kashiwao, fighting against the Court of the South's army - which was commanded by a general named Yoshino Tomonori. Not only was Nobuharu an able soldier; he was also adept in political and civil life. When Nobuharu became the *Shugo* of Kai he faced the restoration of a province drained of resources and ravaged by war. Many soldiers, mostly peasants, had fallen in battle, causing a labor shortage. Social and economic problems could not be properly addressed until peace was established.

Rebellious clans such as the Hemi (Henmi) family and several religious sects had to be dealt with before he could attend to civil matters. They were forced to bow to the rule of the Takeda government or be harshly punished. Once peace was ensured, Nobuharu was able to address the administrative challenges facing the province.

Kai province flourished during his reign, experiencing increased agricultural production, commerce, local industry, arms production and horse breeding. Forts were built along the border with Musashi, and the majority of existing border forts were refurbished in order to ensure military preparedness. Nobuharu also acquired powerful allies during his reign. He contacted the powerful *Kantô kanrei* (Shogunal deputy for the Kantô region), Uesugi Ujinori, and a marriage between his granddaughter and Ujinori sealed the political alliance between the two clans. Unfortunately, this alliance would eventually lead the Kai Takeda into a protracted crisis that nearly destroyed the clan. Nobuharu had sought the alliance, but his son, Takeda Nobumitsu, would pay the price.

When Takeda Nobuharu died in the late autumn of 1413, Nobumitsu became leader of the Takeda clan. There are indications that Nobuharu had retired from public life several years before his death, leaving Nobumitsu to administer the Takeda holdings. It is known that Nobumitsu already held the title of *Shugo* of Kai when Nobuharu passed away. According to one source, this transfer of title took place in 1392; but the records are sketchy, and the date is probably inaccurate. There are strong indications that Nobuharu retired to a manor or a castle at Senno in the 1390's, most likely after 1392. Not only did Nobumitsu inherit his father's titles, but would see the Takeda family brought to the brink of destruction by his daughter's arranged marriage to Ujinori.

Illustration 5

A samurai returning with captured enemy heads. Despite his damaged armor and smears of blood he returns to the main camp in pride. He carries two enemy heads he will present to his lord. The lord's secretary present at camp will record his exploits, and after the battle or campaign ends the warrior, along with his allies, will receive a reward from the lord. The reward could be anything from a sword to landholdings.

CLOSE TO ANNIHILATION

Although several factors led to the fall of the Takeda family, Uesugi Ujinori's uprising proved to be the most destructive. A member of the Inugake Uesugi clan, Uesugi Ujinori had long been in conflict with the Yamanouchi Uesugi clan. Ujinori inherited his clan's territories in 1409, and two years later assumed the title of *Kantô kanrei* after Uesugi Norisada. Norisada, however, had belonged to the Yamanouchi Uesugi clan. As *Kantô kanrei*, Ujinori now served Ashikaga Mochiuji, who was *Kubô* (the *Shôgun's* representative) in Kamakura. The initial spirit of cooperation was soon threatened when Mochiuji declared his loyalty to the Yamanouchi Uesugi clan, led by Uesugi Norimoto. In 1415, Ashikaga Mochiuji confiscated land from one of Ujinori's vassals, Obata Rokurô. Ujinori thought this unjust and, despite his position beneath the *Kubô*, resolved to challenge Mochiuji. In order to do so, he had to recruit allies.

At that time the Ashikaga clan in Kamakura was powerful, both militarily and politically. They could recruit soldiers from across the country, mustering a large army if necessary.

Ujinori approached potential allies, including those with family ties to the Inugake Uesugi clan. Among those approached was, naturally, his father-in-law, Takeda Nobumitsu, to whom he sent a letter explaining his grievances. After consulting with his senior vassals, Nobumitsu agreed that the Takeda clan would support Ujinori. In 1416, Ujinori initiated a rebellion by leading a large army against the Kamakura regime. His main target was Mochiuji's headquarters, where he hoped to find Mochiuji. Ujinori's spies had reported that Mochiuji was living there, and the reports were apparently accurate. Nobumitsu helped lead the attack with his famous Takeda cavalry, and Mochiuji barely managed to escape from the burning headquarters. His fine residence burned to the ground, but after several days' flight, Mochiuji managed to reach Suruga Province. The estate of the *Kantô kanrei*, Uesugi Norimoto, was also attacked and burned to the ground by Ujinori's forces.

TAK 1-19

TAK 1-20

Having narrowly escaped the swords of his enemies, Mochiuji was eager for revenge. He petitioned the central government in Kyôto for assistance. The government in Kyôto naturally considered the attack upon Kamakura as insurrection against the central government. As a result, they issued an order for all the lords in the east to muster troops to put down the revolt in Kamakura. Sources indicate that Nobumitsu was one of Ujinori's most reliable generals and strategic advisors, presumably helping Ujinori plan his campaign. They decided their best chance was to ambush the government forces *en route* to Kamakura. A major confrontation at Kamakura with the greatly superior government army would have been suicidal. Since the enemy was advancing towards Kamakura along two routes, they also decided to divide their forces. They were hoping to surprise the government troops, but Ujinori met a division under the leadership of Imagawa Norimasa (1364-1433), *Shugo* of Suruga, and suffered a crushing defeat.

Takeda Nobumitsu fought the Shin-Echi army near the Seyabara plains. His opponents, from the provinces of Shinano and Echigo, were extremely well disciplined and competent soldiers. They met on January 8th, 1417, before the government army had managed to organize a defense. Nobumitsu stormed the ranks of his enemies like a *tsunami* (tidal wave). His opponents were unable to defend themselves, and the ranks broke as soldiers fled before Nobumitsu's troops. The panic-stricken soldiers were hounded for a considerable period of time before their officers managed to regain control over them. They regrouped and advanced upon Nobumitsu's forces, which were confident and fought like demons. Neither army had apparently lost its will to fight, but once again the government forces were forced to retreat. This time, Nobumitsu's cavalry chased them far into the

photo TAK 1-19 & 1-20

Preparing food while on campaign. One Ashigaru prepares firewood (TAK 1-19), while the other prepares the large iron kettle.

photo TAK 1-21 & 1-22

A representative garden of a temple, shrine, or mansion belonging to a lord or any other within the aristocracy of old Japan. Note the nearly trimmed trees and bushes. The Zen gardens are especially famous for their neatness. It was in such gardens that the samurai could relax and find peace.

neighboring province. When Nobumitsu was satisfied that his opponents had given up, he ordered his troops to return to Kamakura. On the way, Nobumitsu was told that Ujinori had been defeated and forced to commit *seppuku*. Nobumitsu's daughter in Fujiwatari had also committed suicide upon being informed of her husband's death. She is said to have drowned herself.

The news of Ujinori's death forced Nobumitsu to change his plan. He assumed that the *Bakufu* (central government) army had occupied Kamakura, so rather than rushing into the lion's den, he ordered his men back to his headquarters in Kai. If he thought that his troubles were over, he was mistaken. Mochiuji was well aware of Ujinori's accomplices, and intended to make them pay for their treachery.

NOBUMITSU'S DEATH

While awaiting Mochiuji's army, Nobumitsu mobilized his troops. He tried to prepare himself and his people for what was to come. His spies kept him informed of the movements of enemy forces. This allowed him to choose where the battle against Mochiuji would take place.

Ashikaga Mochiuji assigned the task of crushing the Takeda rebellion in Kai to Uesugi Norimune, a Kamakura general. The battle took place on February 3rd, on an open plain north of Mount Fuji. Norimune had around 10,000 men, all adept soldiers. We do not know the number of Nobumitsu's troops, but those he had were well trained and experienced. After the initial confrontation, the line of conflict wavered for several hours. Eventually, the superior numbers of the Kamakura forces began to yield results and Nobumitsu's exhausted soldiers were mowed down. He realized that the battle was lost, and fled to the mountains, along with a handful of survivors. Following a hard march, Nobumitsu and his small entourage came to Mount Tenmokuzan (in the Tokusa Mountains in the Yamanashi district).

On the 6th of February, by the gate of Seiunji Temple, Nobumitsu committed *seppuku*, along with several members of his family and a few vassals. In a single day the powerful Takeda clan was dethroned. This was, to date, the darkest chapter in the history of the clan. Those who survived were forced to flee for their lives. Many Takeda vassals became mercenary

TAK 1-21

TAK 1-22

soldiers, and sought employment with other clans. A few became loggers, others craftsmen. Yet others chose the hazardous but more seductive life of an outlaw, preying on all who traveled through the hinterlands.

Nobumitsu died at Tenmokuzan, but his first-born son, Nobushige, was not present at Seiunji Temple (another source claims that Nobunaga was Nobumitsu's eldest son). When Nobushige heard of his father's death, he knew that he was in grave danger. Fearing for his life, he fled, together with his uncle Nobumoto, to a temple near Mount Kôya. To avoid pursuit, he shaved his head and became a priest. Joining a cloister was a common way to retire from public life and seek anonymity. He took the name Kôzôbô, later calling himself Dôsei. Nobumoto did likewise, assuming the name Kûzan.

Illustration 6

The use of a *naginata*. *Naginata* could be described as a glaive, and here a female samurai uses it to strike at an enemy's knee. She tries to hit him on the back of the knee. If she had struck the front she might have hit the leg protector, and would have been open to counterattack. The *naginata* was the favorite weapon among monks and women. Its origin can traditionally be traced back to the 8th century, but sources indicate its beginnings might be much older. The shaft, typically of oak, was between 1.2 and 1.5 meters in length, but records mention weapons that were 2 meters or more. The blade measured around 0.7 meters, but this length varied considerably from weapon to weapon.

THE HEMI FAMILY

Not all the families in Kai supported the Takeda clan. Some were neutral, and a few supported the Kamakura government, chief among them the Hemi clan. They looked upon Nobumitsu as a traitor, and would have willingly served Nobumitsu's head to Mochiuji on a platter if given the opportunity. Like most other families, they sought power and hoped to gain favor by supporting the Kamakura regime against the Takeda clan.

The Hemi clan had for years contested the authority of the Takeda in Kai, and through Nobumitsu's actions finally glimpsed an opportunity to achieve their goal. Having remained loyal to Ashikaga during the rebellion, they felt that their family had earned the right to assume the title *Shugo* of Kai. The Hemi family now led the vendetta against the Takeda clan, resulting in many years of persecution for the surviving members of the Takeda.

With the two Takeda lords out of the way the stage was set for the Hemi family to exploit the situation. Hemi Arinao went personally to Kamakura to request Mochiuji's support for his petition to be named *Shugo* of Kai. Mochiuji granted him audience, and considered this a good idea. He quickly sent a letter to Kyôto recommending that *Shôgun* Yoshimochi appoint Arinao as *Shugo*. Yoshimochi, however, had no intention of appointing Arinao to this position, and rejected the petition in no uncertain terms. Mochiuji persisted, sending numerous envoys to argue for Arinao's appointment. Despite this, Yoshimochi continued to refuse to grant the petition. Prior to the rebellion, the Takeda clan had been among the *Shôgun's* most loyal subjects, and he felt that the appointment of Arinao would simply create more problems than it would solve. The Hemi were one among many families in Kai and the *Shôgun* knew other families in the province would be upset if the Hemi received the position of *Shugo*, creating even more unrest. He therefore refused to yield to the pressure from the *Kubô* of Kamakura. Eventually, Mochiuji grew tired of arguing, and simply appointed Arinao to the position of *Shugo* himself. The *Shôgun* responded to this maneuver, in 1417 or 1418, by naming the priest (Takeda Nobumoto) Kûzan to the same office, as well as granting him the title of Lord of Mutsu.

After years of unrest in the region Mochiuji was quite unpopular with the central authorities in Kyôto, and became even more so in 1428. In 1423 the fourth *Shôgun*, Yoshimochi, passed his title to his son, Yoshikazu. The young lord was not a man for such an office, and had an unhealthy desire for *sake*. He died in 1425, only 18 years old. After his son's death Yoshimochi was again *Shôgun*, and held the title until his death three years later. After his death his four younger brothers drew lots to determine who would be the new *Shôgun*, with Yoshimitsu's fourth son, Yoshinori, winning the lottery. Mochiuji was infuriated at the way in which the new *Shôgun* had been selected (he thought that he himself should have been appointed) and was at odds with Yoshinori from the start, even to the extent that he considered sending his army against Kyôto. The hostility and confrontations escalated throughout the following decade, leading to the Eikyô rebellion (*Eikyô-no-ran*) from 1438 to 1439.

TAKEDA NOBUMOTO

Let us now return to 1417, when Nobumoto was appointed *Shugo* of Kai while still a priest. It is uncertain whether or not he sought this appointment, but he left the peaceful world of clerical life and returned to the political arena. He moved to the village of Isawa, where he consolidated his position and announced his return to the province. In short order, former vassals of the Takeda clan flocked to the manor offering Nobumoto their services. Once he had assembled the clan's soldiers he revealed his plans. He pointed out that he had yet to deal with certain powerful enemies within the province, particularly the Hemi clan. A military victory against the Hemi would probably have frightened the other clans into submission, but the Hemi clan was so powerful at that time that an open challenge was impractical. Instead, Nobumoto approached the problem from a different direction. He decided to undermine the Hemi clan by bribing or coercing its allies. Ogasawara Masayasu (Nobumoto's nephew) persuaded the Nanbu and Shimoyama clans to join the Takeda faction. With this political maneuver, the Hemi clan lost two crucial supporters in their contest with Takeda, and the balance of power shifted. Upon hearing this information Hemi Arinao realized that he had lost the advantage and would be forced to defend himself. Mobilizing his men, he fortified his borders and awaited Nobumoto's attack.

Before they could attack the Hemi clan, the Nobumoto faction had to tighten its grip on Kai. Nobumoto appointed Atobe Akiumi and his son, Kageie (sometimes spelled Shigeie), to the post of *Shugo-dai*. The *Shugo-dai* substituted for the *Shugo* when he was absent, serving as Nobutomo's advisors and assuming responsibility for the administrative tasks of Kai. The Atobe family were from the Saku district in Shinano province. It is odd that Nobumoto appointed Atobe, as it is unlikely that he was well acquainted with the family. Atobe and his family left Shinano and took up residence in Fuchû, soon distinguishing themselves as skilful administrators. They also had a considerable military force. As often occurred, the ambitious *Shugo-dai* began to oppose the *Shugo* in an attempt to gain power.

During Nobumoto's absence, Atobe used every opportunity to weaken his lord's authority and create unrest. On one occasion, a group of soldiers attacked the village of Komai, which lay on Hemi land. Several of the villagers were killed and the village's store of rice was pillaged. Atobe's soldiers had staged the raid, spreading the rumor that the misdeed had been carried out by Nobumoto's men. When the truth became known, Hemi demanded that the Atobe family should pay for their crime. Nobumoto needed to demonstrate his authority and enforce law and order, but he also wanted to avoid more conflict with the Hemi at this time. He finally decided that the Atobe, both father and son, should travel to Hemi and petition for pardon. Their refusal to do so further strained the ties between the Takeda and Atobe clans. Hemi Arinao, pleased with this outcome, pursued the matter no further.

Shortly thereafter, Nobumoto fell ill. The Atobe family took over all administrative responsibilities and military tasks, and strengthened their influence in Kai. The Hemi clan realized that the Atobe family would soon have full control of the province, and decided to sue for peace before Nobumoto died. Sources are unclear about whether or not peace was achieved. They are also vague concerning the date of Nobumoto's death. A few state that this occurred in 1421, but most prefer 1426. Yoshimochi was still *Shôgun* at the time, and with instability in the eastern provinces becoming a recurring problem he was understandably worried about the possibility of political unrest following Nobumoto's death. He had to decide who should inherit the title of *Shugo*. As we will see later, Nobumoto's nephew, Nobushige, was appointed *Shugo* of Kai in 1423. Unless Nobumoto withdrew from the position because of illness, this would imply that he died before this date.

Illustration 7

The use of a *bô*. Here an *ashigaru* strikes an opponent in the face. The samurai might have thought that this *ashigaru*, only armed with a pole, would be an easy match. Obviously, his attack did not go as planed. The length of the *bô* varied dramatically, from 1.2 meters up to 3 meters or more. One story from the Sengoku period states that the *bô* a tall samurai used was 3.6 meters in length! There also existed shorter variations of *bô*. These were between 20 centimeters and 1.2 meters in length. The *bô* was made of hard wood. mostly oak, or *kunugi* (a kind of oak), and Japanese cedar trees were also used. In some cases it was also strengthened further with strips or bits of iron.

Nobumoto had no children of his own, and had wanted to adopt Nobumitsu's son, Nobunaga. Nobunaga had been one of the ringleaders in Uesugi Ujinori's rebellion against Kamakura and Nobumoto did not wish to provoke Kyôto with the adoption. Instead, Nobumoto adopted Nobunaga's son, Izu Chiyomaru. Nobumoto had hoped that Izu would take over as head of the clan, but things didn't work out as planned.

When Nobumoto died he left no real successor, as Izu was only about four years old. After his death the Atobe clan strengthened its position. It assumed control of the administrative organs and the fortifications that had previously been used by the Takeda family. The situation further deteriorated when the Atobe family kidnapped Izu. Prospects for the Takeda clan seemed dismal, but the Atobe family had not made allowance for a particular Takeda warrior, the boy's father, Takeda Nobunaga.

Ch. 6 – Takeda Nobunaga

NOBUNAGA'S HISTORY

Before we continue, the reader should be acquainted with some details of Nobunaga's life. He was born in 1389, and as a child went under the name of Hachirô. From an early age he was quite like his namesake - Oda Nobunaga (b.1534). Both Nobunagas were given unflattering nicknames. Oda Nobunaga had been called 'Idiot Nobunaga.' Hachirô Nobunaga was called 'Evil Hachirô,' probably behind his back, because of his deplorable conduct. He was apparently unconcerned with the opinion of others and spent most of his time on such favorite pastimes as the martial arts (*bushidô*). Nobunaga was interested in everything related to warfare. He trained hard and long in the use of bow, sword, and spear. He was powerfully built, a giant of a samurai, and used one of the most powerful bows ever made. It is also rumored that he used arrows fashioned from iron. Wherever he went, he attracted attention. After his coming of age ceremony he generally joined his father, Nobumitsu, on military adventures. Amongst these was the Ujinori Rebellion, where Nobunaga distinguished himself as a skilful strategist. In 1417, just before his father committed suicide at Seiunji, Nobunaga fled to Shinano province to seek refuge. He probably did so at his father's request. When circumstances permitted, Nobunaga was expected to re-establish the clan's authority in Kai. In Shinano, Nobunaga was well received by the *Shugo*, Ogasawara Masayasu, who was a very influential person with good contacts. Familial ties between the Takeda and Ogasawara clans ensured that Nobunaga would be protected and hidden from the Kamakura soldiers. Nobunaga remained with his guardians until he heard that the Atobe family intended to execute his son, Izu. Nobunaga decided to rescue his son and finally challenge Atobe. Hastily gathering a few soldiers and journeying to Tsuru, Nobunaga joined forces with Katô Bongen, a local lord.

With a contingent of Bongen's soldiers, Nobunaga journeyed through the Sasago Pass and entered the Yamanashi district. This area belonged to the Hemi and Atobe families. An open confrontation with these enemies would have resulted in defeat, so Nobunaga resorted to guerrilla warfare. Using the advantage of surprise, his soldiers randomly attacked customs stations, small military units, army installations, administrative buildings and supply depots. These raids were effective, and the Hemi and Atobe clans felt constantly threatened. They were also surprised to hear of Nobunaga's presence in the province. They thought he had been killed in battle or had committed suicide in the wake of Ujinori's unsuccessful rebellion. As Nobunaga's exploits became known the size of his forces increased. He was a cunning strategist, as his enemies quickly discovered, and he outwitted them repeatedly.

In addition to the Hemi and Atobe clans, Takeda Nobunaga had other adversaries. The so-called *Rinpô-Ikki* forces resided on Atobe lands, and therefore naturally backed the Atobe clan. The *Ikki* soldiers were basically farmers and lower class warriors that organized themselves into military units. Later on, many members of the *Ikki* joined a highly influential religious sect that turned up during the 1500's. This new sect had a strong religious undertone and later these religious groups were called *Ikkô-Ikki*, which means 'plain thinking.' The *Ikkô-Ikki* belonged to the Jôdo-Shinshû sect of Buddhism. The sect became as powerful as the local lords and contested their authority in the provinces. From the fifteenth century, the central part of Honshû was largely under *Ikkô-Ikki* control. Towards the end of the sixteenth century, Oda Nobunaga had feuded with the numerous *Ikkô-Ikki* temples, heralding their decline.

Takeda Nobunaga also received support from local *Ikki* groups. The so-called *Hi-Ikki* force, which had its base at the Hi-no-jô fort in Nirasaki, had for several decades provided armed support to the Takeda clan. High taxes and other grievances often led to dissatisfaction amongst the *Ikki*, triggering rebellion against their masters. Under the current circumstances, though, Nobunaga welcomed their support. These troops, together with Katô Bongen's men, gradually coalesced into an army. Numbering between 1,000 and 2,000 men the *Hi-Ikki* corps, in combination with Katô's troops and Nobunaga's own men, mustered between 3,000 and 4,000 men. Like most samurai clans, the *Hi-Ikki* forces carried their own *hata-jirushi* flag. This flag displayed a red sun (*Hi* = sun) on a white background. The Takeda family used the same flag, but their flag dated from the eleventh century and was considered to be a clan treasure. Over time, the *Hi-Ikki* forces came to be one of Nobunaga's most important allies, and were given the role of bodyguards.

Attacking the Isawa manor and freeing his son, Izu Chiyomaru, was Nobunaga's first priority. Instead of storming the manor where Chiyomaru was held prisoner, he chose to use *shinobi* (ninja) warriors for this operation. *Shinobi* literally means 'one who steals in.' The *ninja* specialized in stealth and intrusion arts, theft and assassination. The operation was extremely risky: if they were discovered the boy would be killed. Nobunaga naturally wanted to save the life of his son, and was determined to rescue Chiyomaru before he would take further military action against Atobe. Late at night, a small squad of *shinobi* scaled the wall of Atobe's manor. Once over the wall, the squad skillfully stole in and located the boy, whom they found in fine shape. Acting quickly, with the boy between them, the *shinobi* retreated from the manor.

Once the boy was in safe hands, Nobunaga gathered his troops. Now he could challenge Atobe openly. The first major clash between the Atobe and Takeda factions took place by the Arakawa River, which flows through Kôfu Valley. On August 20th, 1421, the two armies fought for several hours. Initially, neither side could win the advantage. Weapons clashed, and the dead and wounded lay strewn along the riverbank. After hours of desperate battle, Atobe's troops began to retreat. Nobunaga declared himself victor, returning with his son to Hi-no-jô in Nirasaki after the heads were counted and the Takeda wounded were tended.

THE FIRST ATTACK

After his defeat at the hands of Nobunaga, Hemi Arinao immediately left for Kamakura to seek an audience with Mochiuji. He told of the conflict in Kai, undoubtedly slanting the account to his own advantage. Mochiuji listened with great interest, and decided that immediate action was necessary. He ordered his general, Yoshimi Norinao, to lead an army of 3,000 men against the revolutionaries. As Yoshimi left Kamakura, Nobunaga's spies informed him that an army was on the way to Kai. Nobunaga thought it would be to his advantage to meet Yoshimi's army on an open battlefield, as a siege would quite likely have ended in his defeat. Nobunaga led his soldiers down to the Kamanashi River, and chose a suitable camp. Yoshimi rode in the vanguard of his army, and halted his troops when he approached the river. He rode unaccompanied down to the riverbank, where he dismounted and announced himself. Nobunaga, who had been watching, stood waiting on the opposite bank, and a dialogue ensued. Nobunaga told Yoshimi of the tyranny of the Hemi and Atobe clans in Kai. His speech must have had the desired effect, because Yoshimi ordered his troops to return to Kamakura in early September. There were apparently no military confrontations between the two camps.

THE SECOND ATTACK

The disturbances in Kai were noted elsewhere in the country. Yoshimochi was following events closely, and was greatly disturbed that a major confrontation had been so narrowly avoided. An armed conflict might have spread to other provinces in the east, and ultimately threatened the Ashikaga hegemony. The *Shôgun* realized that a *Shugo* should be chosen in order to stabilize the province, but the candidate would have to meet the approval of all parties concerned. Yoshimochi knew of Nobushige's withdrawal to Mount Kôya. He had repeatedly sent emissaries to convince Nobushige that he should accept the post of *Shugo*. Nobushige was uninterested, and had politely rejected these requests despite having been nominated to the post in 1423. Yoshimochi eventually turned his attention away from this appointment and on to other matters. The situation remained unchanged for two years, until 1425, when Hemi Arinao once again journeyed to Kamakura to ask Mochiuji for assistance. Once again, Mochiuji agreed to send an army to Kai.

This time, the task fell to Uesugi Mochizane (other source Fusazane). Once again, around 3,000 soldiers were sent against Nobunaga. Nobunaga, who was in Hi-no-jô castle, was kept well informed of the enemy's movements. This time he chose not to meet the enemy in open battle, but clothed himself as a farmer and vanished. Searching for Nobunaga, the Uesugi army came into the Kôfu Valley on the 10th of August 1425. Soldiers searched the buildings in vain - Nobunaga had disappeared without a trace. A few days later, Hemi Arinao arrived with his army to aid in the search, and also established his camp in Kai. Although Hemi Arinao's forces were now in Kai, Mochizane was aware of the threat to himself and his men. He was not only in unfamiliar territory; but the *Hi-Ikki* forces had amassed considerable strength during the last four years. Many were now experienced soldiers, veterans of several years of warfare. Mochizane was uneasy. If the *Hi-Ikki* soldiers should resort to guerrilla warfare against his forces, his troops would suffer high losses. With this belief, he ordered his troops to return to Kamakura on August 17th. Some might have regarded this as dereliction of duty, but he felt that further efforts were pointless, since he could not find Nobunaga. Hemi Arinao remained in Kai a bit longer, but soon realized that the situation was untenable, and returned to his own land as well.

Illustration 8

Using the arm protector. Looking for unprotected areas on the opponent's body, then waiting for the right moment to strike was a typical fighting style for samurai. Sometimes warriors would lure an opponent into exposing his weak points before striking. Here, a samurai parries an enemy strike with his arm, letting the blade hit his arm protector while he uses the opportunity to strike back at the enemy's throat. This was a rather risky maneuver, but when facing a skilled swordsman, sometimes the bravest and most clever warrior would win.

NOBUNAGA ATTACKS

Three days after his enemies had left the province Nobunaga returned from his hiding place in the mountains. As soon as he had come within the palisades of Hi-no-jô Castle he ordered full mobilization. In a few hours the entire province had been alerted, and soldiers began to stream into Kôfu. Samurai, *Hi-Ikki*, and *rônin* (mercenaries) filled Hi-no-jô Castle. When they were assembled, Nobunaga declared, "Now we can attack the Hemi clan."

Nobunaga's first target was the Hemi family's fortress, Wakamiko. The Hemi soldiers, however, were well prepared for the attack, and staged a counter-attack when Nobunaga's troops approached within 30 meters of the walls. What had

begun as a surprise attack quickly turned into a desperate fight for survival. Nobunaga's soldiers held on as long as they could, but the area was soon littered with dead and injured Takeda soldiers. Continuing the attack would have meant total defeat for Nobunaga. He was forced to order a full retreat. Arinao's head would have to wait.

THE THIRD ATTACK

Ashikaga Mochiuji was furious when he heard of Nobunaga's attack on Wakamiko. He ordered Isshiki Mochiie to lead a punitive expedition against Nobunaga. Isshiki was assigned 2,000 elite cavalry soldiers, and an even larger number of infantry. The troops left for Kai early in 1426. For the third time, the Kamakura government was sending an army against Takeda Nobunaga. In the two previous expeditions, Mochiuji's generals had been rather unenthusiastic about following his orders. Nothing indicated that Mochiie would be more successful than the others had been. Instead of vanishing, as he had when Kai was last invaded, Nobunaga chose to confront his adversaries. As usual, Nobunaga's scouts kept him informed of the enemy's movements. Isshiki seemed to be in a hurry, and chose the shortest, fastest route to Kai. The few roads in the area were too narrow to easily accommodate an invading army, allowing one, or perhaps two cavalry soldiers to ride alongside each other. This meant that the army was forced to form a column several kilometers long on its march from Kamakura. At one point, the road passed through a narrow valley, which was an ideal location for an ambush. When Nobunaga heard which route of approach his adversary had chosen, he acted quickly, preparing an ambush before the first scouts reached the valley. Mochiie's army plodded on towards Kai, while Nobunaga's men waited patiently. When Isshiki Mochiie's soldiers were within range of his archers, Nobunaga gave the order to shoot. Isshiki's men dropped like flies while others were lured off the main road, where they were cut down with swords. Soon the survivors were fleeing back down the road, trying to avoid the swords and arrows of the enemy. Once again, Nobunaga had defeated a regiment of elite soldiers. Mochiuji, however, had finally run out of patience.

MOCHIUJI TAKES COMMAND

If Ashikaga Mochiuji was furious at the attack on Wakamiko, he was certainly livid when he learned of Isshiki's defeat. He realized that sending other generals against Nobunaga would be futile, for his officers were simply incompetent. If he intended to succeed, Mochiuji would have to lead the army himself. Naturally, he chose a route to Kai other than that used by Isshiki. He chose to go northeast, through Kobotoke Pass, and invade Kai from the southeast. In preparation for the campaign, Mochiuji had asked the generals from Musashi to mobilize the *Musashi nanatô* (The Seven Lords of Musashi). They were to invade Kai from the Chichibu district in the east, over Gan Pass. Mochiuji intended to attack Nobunaga from two different directions. Perhaps it was not a stroke of genius, but it could work where his generals had failed.

Mochiuji went through the Kobotoke Pass and burned Ôtsuki, an estate in the Tsuru District, to

Illustration 9

Spear fighting. A samurai takes hold of the enemy's spear, and uses the opportunity to rush in at the enemy with his sword. This kind of fighting technique took quite a bit of time and skill to master, but that was what the samurai did – train for battle throughout their lives. One-on-one the foot soldier armed with a spear had no chance against the more skilled samurai.

the ground. A minor skirmish between Mochiuji's troops and Takeda forces took place later that day. For the first time since the battle with the Hemi and Atobe clans, Nobunaga was uncertain about how to tackle the situation and the invading armies marched steadily closer to his camp. His men were prepared for battle, but they faced superior numbers, and presumably felt uncertain about their chances for success. Since they had met the Kamakura soldiers three times earlier, they were aware of the odds. It is probable that many of Nobunaga's men felt that they were doomed. The armies finally clashed in a desperate struggle. After three hours of heroic and bloody resistance, Nobunaga saw that his soldiers were falling in ever-increasing numbers. His men were exhausted, and he realized that the battle was lost. Alone and unarmed, he rode towards Mochiuji's camp. Mochiuji understood that Nobunaga intended to surrender. Ordering his men to let Nobunaga pass, he had his own horse fetched and rode forth to meet his brave adversary. This was a moment that Mochiuji had looked forward to for many years. He beamed as he accepted Nobunaga's capitulation.

Mochiuji let Nobunaga keep his head, but he had to be punished in some way. His punishment was to move to Kamakura, where he was to live out his days serving *Kubô* Mochiuji. With this, Nobunaga became Mochiuji's prisoner. The remaining Takeda soldiers and clan members apparently behaved themselves while Nobunaga was imprisoned in Kamakura. Nobunaga's son, Chiyomaru, was returned to the custody of the Atobe family, who still held the post of *Shugo-dai* of Kai. These events took place in 1426. Nobunaga continued to serve Mochiuji in Kamakura for over five years. His main task seemed fitting: he trained horses. His job was not, however, limited to horses. He also helped train Mochiuji's cavalrymen. Whether he actually enjoyed his new occupation is uncertain, but he apparently did a good job. In April of 1432 he was promoted to supervisor of the building of Daizanji Temple, in Sagami Province.

NOBUNAGA RETURNS

Even after years of service in Kamakura, Nobunaga still dreamed of returning to Kai. Perhaps this was due to his father's desire to have his sons reclaim the hereditary post in Kai; perhaps he still burned with thoughts of revenge against the Atobe. When he became responsible for building the temple of Daizanji, maintaining contact with his allies in Kai became easier. He was apparently allowed a greater

TAK 1-23

TAK 1-24

photo TAK 1-23 & 1-24

These photos show the base of Fuji-*san* over the Yoshida area. It was up along this side of Mount Fuji that Takeda Nobunaga and his small unit made their way back into Kai province in 1433.

degree of freedom, which he quickly exploited. In secret, Nobunaga contacted the *Hi-Ikki* forces in Kai. Twice a month, members of the *tsukaiban* (messenger unit) visited Nobunaga and informed him about events in Kai.

The news was depressing. He was told that the Atobe clan's tyranny continued. Taxes had increased, and those farmers who could not meet their obligations were seriously mistreated, even tortured. The villagers had no higher authority to which they could bring their grievances; they were entirely at the mercy of the Atobe clan. Worst of all, there were new rumors that Izu Chiyomaru was to be killed. Chiyomaru was rapidly approaching the age at which he would participate in the ceremony in which he would become a samurai. Opponents of the Atobe clan might well view the young samurai as a potential leader, who would then present a threat to the Atobe family's autonomy. Nobunaga was aware of the situation, but as long as he was confined to Kamakura, there was little that he could do. In early March of 1433, Nobunaga secretly left Kamakura, bound for Kai. He was understandably somewhat concerned about how his small band would enter the province unnoticed. Since the Atobe clan's scouts were constantly out patrolling, Nobunaga thought it best to make a detour.

Together with Kudô Yaheiji and six other close friends, Nobunaga left Kamakura and swung westwards towards Hakone. He and his group of confederates continued on north to Kagosaka Pass, near Mount Fuji. They left the mountains and went towards Lake Yamanaka, and with the lake on their right side and Mount Fuji to the left the small group continued their march. When the group came to Yoshida, they turned westward towards Lake Kawaguchi. Following the road towards Misaka to Ôishi Pass, they established a camp on Mount Hanatori. The *Hi-Ikki* had been informed of Nobunaga's arrival, and around 50 of them met the little group as they arrived at Hanatori. The *Hi-Ikki* soldiers had been very careful not to disclose their movements to the enemy by coming in small groups of two to three men.

As soon as Nobunaga was within the borders of Kai and safe among his own relatives, he ordered full mobilization. His goal was to once again free Chiyomaru from the Atobe stronghold. The boy was living at the former Takeda estate, Isawa. The *Hi-Ikki* force grew rapidly and prepared for battle. The Atobe and Hemi clans were fully aware of Nobunaga's arrival, but were uncertain of his whereabouts. Both knew they would be challenged, and agreed to support each other when the armed struggle began. They had no illusions about their fate if Nobunaga should win the battle. They knew that the Atobe and Hemi clans would be destroyed.

photo TAK 1-25

Lake Kawaguchi - picture taken from top of Mount Tenjô. The valley that cuts to the left in the background leads up to the Ôishi Mountain Pass. It was at this pass that Takeda Nobunaga and his unit crossed over into Kôfu valley in 1433.

WAR AGAINST THE ATOBE AND HEMI CLANS

Nobunaga and his *Ikki* troops were then about 10 kilometers from the Isawa estate. Late that evening they held a conference to plan their strategy. The meeting was followed by a meal of *imogayu* (rice pudding), pork and finally *ume* (apricots) before they began their march from Mount Hanatori. Their highest priority was to free Chiyomaru before his enemies could injure him. It was possible that they were already too late. The cavalrymen gently led their mounts down towards the Fuefuki River, careful to keep the horses quiet, so that they would not be heard. This took considerable time, and it was nearly sunrise before the unit reached the riverbank.

The troop of roughly 60 men waded the river slowly, so that they would not be detected, and cautiously approached the main gate. Scouts had already neutralized the estate's lookouts. When the troops were about a meter from the gate, Nobunaga began the attack. Some foot soldiers attached a pair of hooks to the gate, and horses were used to tear it down. Fully armed soldiers with swords and short spears stormed into the courtyard and engaged the half-naked Atobe soldiers stumbling out of the buildings with swords in hand, half asleep. Nobunaga's men easily slaughtered the unorganized and poorly armed defenders. A small party of *Hi-Ikki* soldiers were ordered to find Chiyomaru, while the main troop continued mowing down the enemy. Atobe Akiumi and his son barely managed to escape out a back door of the main building, just ahead of Nobunaga's soldiers. They fled into the woods and disappeared. The unit searching for Chiyomaru fought its way into the next courtyard, where they discovered the boy in one of the buildings; once again, amazingly uninjured.

A half-hour later, the battle for Isawa was over. Nobunaga was delighted over the outcome of the battle. The heads of over 100 Atobe soldiers were collected and only four of his men had been injured; none had died. He glowed with joy when Chiyomaru was brought to him. After seven long years, father and son were finally reunited. Of course, the *Hi-Ikki* soldiers had not been forgotten. All were praised for their contributions to the battle. Nobunaga's only disappointment was that Atobe Akiumi had escaped. If the Takeda forces had managed to take Akiumi's head, the war might have ended right there. Since they had not done so, Nobunaga knew that his stay must be short. He asked his soldiers to prepare to disband. His immediate task was to determine his next move against the Hemi and Atobe clans. He planned to do so within the palisades of Hi-no-jô Castle.

How did the Kamakura government react to Nobunaga's flight? It appears that Nobunaga's colleagues in Mochiuji's court defended Nobunaga's actions. Whatever the reason, Mochiuji did not react. Perhaps Mochiuji had finally begun to understand the situation in Kai, and had realized that Nobunaga's struggle against the Atobe and Hemi clans was justified, or that his own influence at court was beginning to wane.

THE BATTLE AT ARAKAWA

Illustration 10

Spear fighting. A samurai steps on the opponent's spear while he thrusts his own into the enemy's abdomen - a painful death.

Nobunaga and his son returned to Hi-no-jô, arriving on March 4th, 1433. A jubilant population who hoped that the misrule of the Atobe clan would soon be over greeted them. Nobunaga enjoyed a pleasant reunion with other members of the clan at Hi-no-jô castle. Unfortunately this respite did not last. His chief enemy, Atobe Akiumi, was mobilizing his troops, as was the Hemi family.

Takeda Nobunaga and his men remained within the walls of Hi-no-jô castle for nearly two months. Throughout this time, Atobe attempted unsuccessfully to lure Nobunaga into open battle. Atobe's army of roughly 2,000 men eventually returned to Isawa without realizing this objective. Nobunaga knew that a decisive battle with Atobe and Hemi was unavoidable. His options were few; either linger within the protective walls of the castle, or meet his adversaries on open battlefield. After careful consideration, he decided to take the initiative. On the morning of April 29th, Nobunaga ordered his men to prepare for the crucial battle. Early in the afternoon, he and his troops marched out of Hi-no-jô castle, heading for Tomi, a hill south of Hi-no-jô. After climbing the hill, they made camp on the bank of the Arakawa River.

By the time Nobunaga and his men marched out of Hi-no-jô Castle, Atobe Akiumi had already left Isawa with his army. This mobilization was based on the information provided by Atobe's *shinobi*, who continually reported to their leader on Nobunaga's movements. The Hemi clan allied with the Atobe clan, agreeing to reinforce Atobe's troops with Hemi and *Rinpô Ikki* forces. Atobe's army passed Fuchû and reached the Arakawa River in the late afternoon. Atobe found Nobunaga's troops already in position when his troops approached the opposite bank.

The two armies advanced towards the riverbanks; and as the infantry clashed Nobunaga led his cavalry deep into enemy ranks. He had underestimated the Atobe soldiers, who fought valiantly and held their position. Enemy infantry and cavalry soon surrounded Nobunaga's men. The dramatic attack had turned into a desperate defense for the Takeda forces. Exhaustion set in as the day wore on and Nobunaga, with Chiyomaru at his side, ordered a retreat. Kudô Yaheiji and three others, who had been with Nobunaga since his flight from Kamakura, had fallen in battle and had to be left behind. Many of the *Hi-Ikki* forces were also slain. Nobunaga and his son managed to reach Hi-no-jô, but were not yet safe from Atobe's men. He decided to proceed to Shinano, where Ogasawara Masayasu ruled. Masayasu welcomed the weary fugitives with open arms, but the relationship quickly cooled. Since Masayasu was *Shugo* of Shinano, his primary loyalty was to the *Bakufu* and the Kamakura government. Giving shelter to Nobunaga threatened his relationship with the Kamakura *Kubô*. Fortunately for Masayasu, Nobunaga and his son soon left Shinano and headed for Suruga before a decision had to be made.

KYÔTO

The entire episode caused heated debate between the central government in Kyôto and the Kamakura regime. This could have led the entire region into civil war, if it had been allowed to continue. *Shôgun* Yoshinori had no desire to escalate a relatively minor conflict into a major confrontation, but Mochiuji precipitated the most acute problem. Upon learning of Nobunaga's presence in Suruga, Mochiuji asked Yoshinori for permission to send a punitive expedition to the province. On the 6th of June, Yoshinori summoned the lords to a meeting of the Council to discuss the situation. Mochiuji's proposal was discussed but ultimately rejected. Yoshinori decided it was best to resolve the conflict peacefully. It seems that in an effort to end the conflict Yoshinori took Nobunaga under his wing and made the Takeda a sort of *tozama* (outside vassal). In addition, to take care of Nobunaga and his son, Yoshinori gave Nobunaga a village in Tôtômikaba worth 1,000 *kanmon* to administer. For a time, this village became Nobunaga's home, but seeking refuge in a neutral province did not provide much protection; his enemies could track him down wherever he might hide. He knew that his life hung by a thread, but there was hope, however, for his son, Izu Chiyomaru. He would be safe in Kyôto. Nobunaga almost begged *Shôgun* Yoshinori to take care of the boy until the conflict with Mochiuji was resolved. He also had an opportunity to relate the entire story of the Atobe clan's misdeeds in Kai. *Shôgun* Yoshinori listened to Nobunaga's explanation and recognized the injustice that the Takeda clan had suffered at the hands of the Atobe family. Nobunaga and Izu Chiyomaru were both granted permission to reside in Kyôto under the *Shôgun's* protection.

On the 2nd of July 1434, on a very hot afternoon, a troop of 100 cavalrymen attacked Isawa Manor. Only soldiers were present at the manor when it was attacked. Atobe Akiumi and his family were at their summer residence in Mitomi. A violent skirmish took place at the gates of the manor, an alarm was raised, and *Rinpô Ikki* forces rushed from nearby villages.

Joining the soldiers in the manor, they managed to repulse the attack. As soon as Atobe Akiumi received news of the attack he returned to Isawa, discussing with his officers who might have staged it. Takeda Nobunaga was naturally first among the suspects, but Atobe Akiumi thought that Nobunaga was still in Suruga. Had he managed to return to Kai unnoticed? Atobe never resolved this riddle, but Nobunaga was most probably one of the ringleaders behind the attack, since Atobe had no other enemies in Kai capable of mounting such an assault.

Preparing for batle, a samurai fastens *his hachimaki* (headband) before donning his *kabuto* (helmet).

THE EIKYÔ REBELLION

In 1438 Nobunaga and Izu Chiyomaru were still in the service of *Shôgun* Yoshinori in Kyôto. Ashikaga Mochiuji had taken issue with his vassal Uesugi Norizane, and the latter gathered what he could of allies when he heard that Mochiuji was preparing to send an army against him. Uesugi Norizane knew that he had a possible ally in Kyôto and appealed to *Shôgun* Yoshinori for assistance. Imagawa Noritada, Ogasawara Masayasu, the Takeda family, and others were ordered to assist Norizane in his struggle with Mochiuji. The *Shôgun* viewed this as an opportunity to curtail Mochiuji's impulsive behavior. On the 14th of February 1439, Norizane's allies, Chiba Tanenao and Uesugi Mochitomo, attacked Yôanji temple in Kamakura, where Mochiuji and his family resided. Several members of Mochiuji's clan were killed or committed *seppuku* in the heat of battle. Mochiuji followed the advice of Uesugi Norizane's vassal, Nagao Tadamasa, and withdrew from public life. He shaved his head and became a priest. He had difficulty adjusting to his new way of life, and after a few months he also committed *seppuku*. According to Japanese custom, he left the world of the living with his honor intact. The possibility that peace might finally be established in eastern Japan was, however, soon crushed by the appearance of a new rebel.

TAK 1-26

TAK 1-27

THE YÛKI REBELLION

The new militant was Yûki Ujitomo, the Lord of Yûki Castle in Shimosa province, who had instigated a rebellion against Kyôto. Three of Mochiuji's sons, Haruômaru, Yasuômaru and Eijuômaru, had survived the attack on Yôanji, and Yûki Ujitomo had taken the three boys under his wing. Eijuômaru was only three years old when his father committed *seppuku* and was sent to Ôi Mochimitsu in the district of Shinshû, where he achieved fame as Ashikaga Shigeuji. Other generals took in the two older sons, but after a while they returned to Yûki Ujitomo in Yûki. Once Ujitomo had two of Mochiuji's sons within the walls of his castle, he revolted against the Kyôto government and raised the flag of rebellion.

Takeda Nobushige had finally returned from his clerical life and accepted the mantle of leader of the Takeda clan in 1428. Together with his younger brother, Nobunaga, he fought under Ogasawara Masayasu, who was appointed commander-in-chief by Yoshinori in the campaign against Yûki Ujitomo. There was no quick solution to the problem of the Yûki clan. For nearly a year Yûki Ujitomo managed to repel the *Bakufu* army, but when some of his most crucial allies changed sides and joined forces with the enemy, his rebellion was doomed.

In April 1441 a decisive attack was launched against Yûki. After a long and heroic battle, Ujitomo finally had to acknowledge defeat, and he committed *seppuku* together with several close family members and vassals. Mochiuji's three sons were in the castle when it fell. They were taken prisoner and were to be sent to the capital, but on the way two were done away with. For reasons unknown, Eijuômaru's life was spared and the following year he was sent to Kyôto.

TAKEDA NOBUNAGA'S FINAL YEAR

Takeda Nobunaga served under Yoshinori up until the *Shôgun's* death in 1441. Later, he served under the new Kamakura *Kubô*, Ashikaga Shigeuji (in some sources the name is written Nariuji), Ashikaga Mochiuji's surviving son (who by this time had changed his name from Eijuômaru). In January 1456 he set off with an army for Kazusa Province, where he restored Marigayatsu (Mariyatsu) Castle. This had once belonged to the Chônan clan, and was now to serve as headquarters for the Bôsô district, along with Chônan Castle, also under the jurisdiction of the Bôsô branch of the Takeda family. Nobunaga took up residence in the castle with his son, Izu Chiyomaru. Before long, the founder of the Kazusa Takeda clan, Takeda Nobunaga, was promoted. He was given the position of *Shugo-dai* of the province in which he now resided. Unfortunately, Nobunaga's period as *Shugo-dai* was brief; he died in March 1457, just over a year after moving to Kazusa Province. Some sources say that he lived to an age of 67 or 68 years. Chiyomaru's name changed to Nobutaka after his *genpuku* ceremony. His oldest son, Nobuoki, changed his family name to Marigayatsu Nobuoki after his *genpuku* ceremony. Takeda Nobutaka's second son, Tokinobu, inherited land and property in Kai, as well as the Ichijô family name, changing his own to Ichijô Genpachi Tokinobu.

Illustration 11

Use of the *kama-yari* or *magari-yari* (yari = spear). Here a samurai is holding a *kama-yari* ready for action. The sketch shows the position of the blade in defense (*hiragama*) above and in offensive (*kirikama*) stance below. Used in defense, the blade was held flat to stop incoming sword, *naginata* or spear strikes. It is believed that it first appeared during the Kamakura period, 12th century. The *kama-yari* was usually much shorter then an ordinary spear. But the length of the shaft grew during the Sengoku period to around 2 meters with a 40-centimetre blade. During the Edo period the weapon grew to 2.4 meters in length for the shaft, and 40 to 50 centimeters for the blade, while the cross-blade ranged between 20 to 30 centimeters in length. Several variations of this weapon existed during the 15th and 16th centuries.

Ch. 7-The Treachery of the Atobe

TAKEDA NOBUSHIGE RETURNS TO KAI

After Uesugi Ujinori's rebellion in 1416, Nobushige had abandoned worldly affairs to become a Buddhist priest. A new chieftain had also been chosen for the Takeda clan. A new *Shugo* of Kai was required and only Yoshimochi, the *Shôgun* in Kyôto, had the authority to make such an appointment. After seeking council, he appointed Takeda Nobumoto, who was now living as a priest on Mount Kôya. Nobumoto, a younger brother of Nobumitsu, had not participated in the Ujinori Rebellion. He was therefore an excellent and logical candidate for the position of *Shugo*.

Nobumoto had a turbulent period as *Shugo* and after a few years a new *Shugo* was needed. The *Shôgun* chose Nobushige, who refused to leave Kôya. After several years of pressure from the *Shôgun* Nobushige finally moved out of the temple area, but didn't return to Kai. Instead he was granted two villages in Suruga province. Nobushige did not hide in Suruga; on the contrary, he traveled around and on one occasion was granted an audience with *Shôgun* Yoshinori, being honored with a pair of excellent swords. Although Nobushige had received the letter verifying him as *Shugo* of Kai while at Kôya in 1423, it would not be until 1438 that he would return to his home province.

At Yoshinori's request, *Shugo* Nobushige led a force of 2,000 men against Kai. His goal was straightforward. He was to capture Isawa and depose the Atobe clan. Atobe Akiumi heard of Nobushige's plans, and realized that further co-operation with the Kamakura regime was inadvisable. He avoided all further contact with Kamakura and surrendered to the new *Shugo* without resistance. Ogasawara Masayasu, who was now supporting Nobushige, gave the Atobe clan a reprimand that echoed throughout the province.

Many challenges still remained after the issue of the Atobe clan had been settled. The inhabitants of the province had suffered heavily under tyrannical rule, and many difficulties had to be overcome before the people would trust a new lord. The overall situation, however, seemed promising. The populace had waited many years for the Takeda clan to free Kai from the yoke of the Atobe. When the Takeda finally arrived, they received the whole-hearted support of the population. Takeda Nobushige began the construction of a new manor, which he called Koisawa (little Isawa). The structure was completed in three months, and Nobushige moved in. Ashikaga Mochiuji, who did not

TAK 1-28

TAK 1-29

intend to let Nobushige's appointment remain uncontested, observed these activities with consternation. Again, the Kyôto and Kamakura regimes wavered on the brink of war. *Shôgun* Yoshinori was determined to hinder Mochiuji from expanding his area of mobilization. In order to taunt Mochiuji, he gave Nobushige two villages, Sano and Sawata, on the border between the provinces of Sagami and Suruga. Yoshinori then had allies on Mochiuji's doorstep.

Several of the ideas that guided the Takeda clan seem to have originated with a high priest by the name of Mansai (1378-1435). He served the *Bakufu* government and was a man of considerable power, belonging to one of the *Kugyô*-families who served the Emperor. *Kugyô* means 'court family of the highest rank,' and his position gave him influence with powerful members of the Emperor's Court. Mansai apparently knew how to exploit such connections, since he appears to have swayed many of the decisions made by Yoshimochi and Yoshinori with respect to the Takeda family. It is difficult to corroborate Mansai's reputed efforts to promote the Takeda clan, but his diary is the main source of the Takeda family's history from the time of the Ujinori rebellion in 1416 to Mansai's death in 1435.

Takeda Nobushige was now satisfied that the Atobe clan had surrendered without resistance, and a peace treaty was signed between the two families. The Hemi clan was now his only remaining adversary in Kai. It is uncertain whether the Hemi clan actually surrendered to the Takeda clan, but some sources mention that they were rendered harmless at this time.

photo TAK 1-28 & 1-29

Ashigaru on a lunch-break while on campaign. They all wear simple *tatami-gusoku* (folding armor). In the background stand two *tate* (shields) bearing the *oshiki ni nami sanmoji* crest. Also visible are the *maku* curtains the army has set up around the camp.

In 1441 Nobushige participated in the attack on Yûki in Shimosa province. In this battle Nobushige's men had taken the heads of Yûki Shichirô and Yûki Jirô, as well as five other Yûki clan members, and he returned to Kai after the successful campaign. To celebrate *Shôgun* Yoshinori's victory over Yûki, festivities were held on the evening of August 14th at Akamatsu Mitsusuke's manor in Kyôto. As the evening wore on, everyone drank, feasted, and made merry - until a tragic event took place. In the presence of the guests the *Shôgun* was cut down. The assassination was planned by Akamatsu Mitsusuke to express his violent displeasure at being refused the position of *Shugo* of Harima province. In Kai, word of Yoshinori's death spread quickly, and a punitive expedition against the culprit was organized. Nobushige naturally took part in the foray. The Yamana clan was given most of the credit for the military reprisals against Akamatsu, but several other clans also took part in the campaign. Among these were Ogasawara, Imagawa, the Kai Takeda and the Aki Takeda (under the leadership of Takeda Nobukata). In a few days, Kinoyama, Akamatsu Mitsusuke's castle in Harima, was surrounded by enemy troops. As soon as the *Bakufu* forces were in position, they were ordered to attack. The outcome of the battle was a foregone conclusion. Mitsusuke's men fought bravely, but they were vastly outnumbered. The defense was eventually crushed, and Mitsusuke and his clan were slaughtered.

About a year after Ashikaga Yoshinori's assassination Ogasawara Masayasu died after a brief illness, and Nobushige lost yet another of his long-time supporters. Takeda Nobushige was saddened immeasurably when he heard the news, and attended the funeral with a heavy heart. Debate over the choice of a new clan chieftain immediately broke out among Ogasawara Masayasu's heirs. Masayasu's son, Muneyasu, seemed the most logical candidate, but Mochinaga, who came from the Fuchû Ogasawara line, soon challenged him to the title. A battle on Urushidahara plain in 1446, in which Muneyasu was killed, decided the contest and Mochinaga was the winner. Unfortunately, his victory was short-lived and did not provide him with any real political power.

NOBUSHIGE'S DEATH

Shortly after Masayasu's funeral, Nobushige experienced other difficulties. The problematic Atobe and Hemi clans had been neutralized, but new clans began to hoist the flag of rebellion. One of these rebels, Kurosaka Jirô, lived in a narrow valley close to where the town of Sakaigawa now stands. The motives for his rebellion are unclear, but the desire for more land and power, and displeasure over high taxes, probably played a role. Backed by local bands of farmer-soldiers, he started an *Ikki*-rebellion. Nobushige was informed of the situation by his *shinobi,* and he and his men girded themselves once again for battle. While he was on his way to Sakaigawa, his Koisawa manor was attacked and burned to the ground by the lord of Oyama Castle, Anayama Izu no Kami. Anayama's soldiers slaughtered Nobushige's family, including the women and children. Nobushige's *shinobi* caught up with their lord before he reached Sakaigawa and told him the appalling news. Ashen with fury, he turned abruptly and set out for home, bent on revenge. Anayama had anticipated this rash reaction, and had ordered his soldiers to ambush Nobushige and his men as they passed. When Nobushige galloped straight into the arms of the enemy, Anayama's soldiers rushed out from the thicket, surrounding him. He defended himself as well as possible, holding the enemy at bay by jabbing and thrusting with his spear. As he became exhausted, he realized that his time had come. With his right hand he took his *tantô* (dagger) and plunged it into his breast. With blood streaming from the deep wound, Nobushige fell from his horse. One of the greatest Takeda clan warriors was gone forever.

TAKEDA NOBUMORI

Takeda Nobushige had been ambushed and killed by Anayama's men on the afternoon of November 24th, 1450. Like his father, Nobushige had died tragically; but unlike his father, Nobushige had accomplished many of the goals his father had set forth. The Atobe and Hemi clans had been pacified, and the Takeda clan was once again a powerful force in the province of Kai.

The next Takeda clan chieftain was Nobushige's son, Nobumori, who had escaped capture by Anayama's soldiers in the ambush. Although references are sparse, it is believed that he sought shelter in the manor of his mother's family, Oyamada. Taking up the reins of leadership his father had left him posed a difficult challenge for Nobumori, for he would have to continue expanding the power and influence of the Takeda clan. Nobumori was appointed *Shugo* of Kai, a position he held until his death a mere five years later. After Koisawa Manor had burned down, Nobumori built a new manor in the district of Yatsushiro, where he spent his remaining years. From this new base he led the entire Takeda clan in a punitive expedition against Anayama Izu no Kami and Kurosaka Jirô in which both were neutralized. Nobumori, plagued by illness throughout his life, died in May 1455. He left a son and heir, Nobumasa, but the boy was only nine years old. With a chieftain too young to lead them, the Takeda were once again threatened by a renewed Atobe clan.

TAKEDA NOBUMASA

Two days before his death, Nobumori spoke with his son Nobumasa. He told Nobumasa that he would soon die, and that the grave responsibility of leading the clan would now be placed squarely on his young shoulders. He also warned his son that as long as the Atobe clan existed, they would pose a constant threat to the House of Takeda, telling him that he must never forget the misdeeds of the Atobe, to be constantly on guard, and to keep a close eye on the activities of the Atobe clan.

Atobe Akiumi had withdrawn from public life and turned over the helm to his son, Kageie. Like his father, Kageie was a deceitful leader. Immediately after Nobumori's death Kageie wrote a letter to Kyôto proposing that he should be appointed as Nobumasa's guardian until the boy was old enough to lead the Takeda clan himself. *Shôgun* Yoshimasa accepted the proposition and sent a letter, with his signature, as proof that Kageie should be given responsibility for the boy. Yoshimasa accepted this request probably because he was unaware of the situation in Kai and the ongoing conflict between the Takeda and Atobe clan. Kageie then had to convince Nobumasa's vassals that he should be the boy's legal guardian. He must have been adept in the art of persuasion, because there was no confrontation at the time. However, Kageie's subsequent actions were foolish, and soon led to discord between the families.

MIHATA AND THE TATENASHI-NO-YOROIARMOR

Ever since the time of Shinrasaburô (1057-1127), the Takeda clan had kept two family clenodiums in their possession: the first was *Mihata* (the red sun flag) and the second was *Tatenashi-no-yoroi* (the armor of Shinrasaburô Yoshimitsu). These two objects were considered to be the clan's two most valuable possessions and were symbols of the family's origin and success. Atobe Kageie claimed that he had the right to guard these family treasures as long as Nobumasa was his ward, and therefore had them moved from Yatsushiro to Isawa. His audacity was the last straw for Nobumasa and his vassals. Kageie's actions were an unforgivable insult and could not be tolerated; thirteen year-old Nobumasa ordered his men to repossess the treasures by force. On the 28th of December 1457, Nobumasa's forces attacked the village of Isawa. Evidence seems to indicate that Atobe was forewarned. When Nobumasa's men stormed the village, they met powerful resistance and suffered heavy losses. Ultimately, they were repelled by the defenders and were forced to retreat leaving many of their fallen strewn on the battlefield. The attack had been an impulsive reaction to the Atobe's insult, and was poorly organized. The reputed losses were so high that the statistics themselves seem questionable.

This did not seem to dissuade Nobumasa from making a second attempt. The following year, on January 8th, a new assault was launched on Isawa. This attack also failed miserably. In this attack all the male members of the Iwasaki family, who were Takeda retainers, were wiped out. After two bitter defeats, the Takeda clan had to admit that they could not yet defeat the Atobe. They chose to wait for more favorable circumstances.

Several years passed without major confrontations between the two families. Prior to his *genpuku* Nobumasa had been called Gorô, and after the ceremony he assumed his adult name, Takeda Nobumasa. *Shôgun* Yoshimasa named him as *Shugo* of Kai, giving him the title *Gyôbudaiyû*. Unsurprisingly, the Atobe did not return the family relics once Nobumasa reached his majority. But now the Takeda clan once again ruled Kai and the recovery of the relics became a clan imperative. After his father's death young Nobumasa had begun to study the art of war, as did all samurai. He had survived a period of illness, and was now a strong young man. He had acquired allies such as Anayama Nobusuke and Imai Nobutsune, two powerful generals who strengthened his authority in Kôfu. Nobumasa also forbade Atobe Kageie to trespass on Takeda land, which made his attitude toward the Atobe clan known, even if he did not directly declare war on Kageie. A sort of 'cold war' followed, and both families prepared for the inevitable war each knew was coming. In February 1464 the death of Kageie's father, Akiumi, shook the family. Even though Akiumi had officially retired several years earlier, he had always supported his son and family from behind the scene. His death was a hard blow to Kageie.

The Takeda family was also having problems of its own with enemies from outside the province. Ambitious lords sought to steal land while the political situation in the province was unstable. Suwa Nobumitsu joined forces with the Ôi clan, and invaded Kai in April of 1464. What happened afterwards is unclear, but there were many such opportunists, and it was imperative that Nobumasa quickly establish an effective government in his home province. This meant dealing with Atobe Kageie.

Nobumasa set about recruiting allies for the battle. Among these were the Anayama, Imai, Yukawa, and Oyamada clans, as well as troops from Suwa in Shinshû. In June 1465, with a following of 2,000 cavalry, and probably twice that many infantry, Nobumasa set out for Isawa Village. En route, he had to pass a small fort, which would normally have been a minor inconvenience - but it was here that Kageie had chosen to make his stand. Nobumasa decided that the battle might just as well be fought there as in Isawa Village, and ordered his soldiers to take up battle positions. Clothed in the appropriated *Tatenashi-no-yoroi* armor, Kageie climbed onto a turret and gazed upon the enemy troops. When he located Nobumasa, he shouted, "Nobumasa! If you want this armor, you will have to take it by force!" Nobumasa accepted the challenge and called upon his best

Illustration 12

The use of *naigama* (also know as *mohazushi*). A fierce battle rages, and the samurai armed with a *naigama* siezes the opportunity to strike at the opponent's neck. It was originally a farmer's tool, but when needed it could be used as a lethal weapon. This tool's origin goes back to China, but is was in use in Japan until the 16th century, mainly by farmers in so called *Ikki* units. It was used with great effect on cavalry soldiers - pulling the enemy from horseback. The navy also used it, but not always as a weapon. Sailors could use the *naigama* to remove unwanted obstacles such as sea-grass tangled in a boat's rudder. The average shaft length was around 3 meters, while the hooked blade ranged between 10 centimeters and 30 centimeters.

archer. "Shoot him!" he cried. The archer sighted and loosed the arrow. Kageie fell from the tower, but his men quickly carried him to safety. They removed the suit of armor and left it behind in their retreat to Otanoyama. When Nobumasa's men entered the fort they retrieved the armor, recovering one of the family treasures stolen by the Atobe. Nobumasa was more than satisfied with the outcome of the confrontation, and left nearly 500 men to defend the fort. The rest of his army returned to Yatsushiro. The fate of the flag is not mentioned, but it is assumed that it was recovered when Kageie's men fled.

THE FALL OF THE ATOBE CLAN

Kageie had been sorely injured by the arrow, but not fatally. When Nobumasa realized that his hated enemy was going to survive, he mobilized his army once again. He intended to finish Kageie off, and wipe out the family that had been a plague to the Takeda clan for nearly half a century. By July the Takeda army was once again on the march, Nobumasa's spies reporting that Kageie was in Otanoyama fort. His army attacked the fort's outer defenses, taking them easily; and when the troops were in position, Nobumasa gave an order to storm the inner defenses. The Takeda army poured over the walls, seizing the fort in a short but vicious battle. Kageie, badly wounded, was captured along with seven of his vassals. He was escorted to Nobumasa's headquarters where he was made to kneel and commit *seppuku* on the riverbank below his own fort, as Nobumasa gazed without compassion upon him. Thus ended almost 50 years of Atobe tyranny.

Ch. 8 – New Dilemmas

THE BEGINNING OF THE ÔNIN WAR

In December 1465 new storm clouds appeared on the horizon. However, these impending difficulties involved higher echelons of government and not local discord, as they so often had in the past. *Shôgun* Yoshimasa was having problems with the Koga *Kubô*, Ashikaga Shigeuji. The *Shôgun* ordered Nobumasa and Imagawa Yoshitada to march on Shigeuji, with Nobumasa setting off in March 1466 with a force of 3,000 cavalry. The army crossed into Shinano Province, coming out onto a plateau-like plain belonging to Shigeuji, though actually occupied by one of his allies, a lord called Murakami Masakuni.

Winter was not the best time of year to invade Shinano. The snow was already deep, and it continued to fall. The bitter cold and deep snows made marching difficult; and as the army crossed the plain, Nobumasa felt that there was something amiss. His suspicions were confirmed when a shower of arrows rained down on his forces. "Down in the snow!" he shouted. His men threw themselves down so that they were nearly covered with snow, laying motionless. This was actually a rather clever idea, since it left the enemy with no targets. Bereft of targets for their archers, the enemy abandoned the protection of the forest and approached Nobumasa and his men, who were waiting with drawn swords. When the enemy had approached to within a few meters, Nobumasa sprang up and ordered his men to attack. Shortly, the entire area became a chaotic mass of men fighting fanatically with swords and spears. Winter days are short, and darkness fell quickly, but this did not deter the combatants, with the battle continuing on through the evening. Finally, Nobumasa pulled his men back from the plain and camped for the night. The enemy had also suffered heavy losses and decided to retreat; the following day, Nobumasa returned to the battlefield to find almost 500 fallen samurai.

After this battle there was but a short respite before new hostilities broke out. These conflicts and the Ônin War will be described in the second book in this series.

I have chosen to end the first book here, on the threshold of a new era, which was a turning point in Japanese history. This period, known as the Ônin War, will be the basis of the second book. The Ônin war began in 1467 and ended officially in 1477, but was actually the beginning of a conflict that threw the entire country into anarchy for the following century.

Aki Province	The Aki Province is now known as the Hiroshima prefecture.
Bakufu	The seat of the Kamakura government - the Shogunate.
Edo Period	The period between 1603 and 1867.
fudai	This word could be translated as "insiders." These were vassals who were considered faithful, and were therefore members of their lord's inner circle. Those vassals who were not members of the inner circle were called *tozama*, or "outsiders."
genpuku	A ceremony in which a boy is initiated into the world of adults (a coming-of-age ceremony).
Ikki	A group of farmers and low-class samurai that joined together in armed units.
ji-samurai	Samurai who owned some land or governed a small area, and who served under a powerful feudal lord.
Jitô	A steward - the lord of a manor.
_____ no *Kami*	Lord over (of) a province. (Kai no Kami).
Kamakura	A city located southwest of Tokyo. It was the seat of the Kamakura Bakufu from 1192 until 1333.
kanja	Young man. Takeda kanja – "the young Takeda."
Kantô kanrei	Shogunal deputy for the Kantô region - present day Tokyo area.

ken	In Japanese, a prefecture is called "ken," hence "Yamanashi-ken" is "Yamanashi prefecture."
Kiyohara	A family name which is spelled Kiyowara in some books.
kunishû	Farmers and minor landed samurai who served in rural regiments.
Kyôto	One of the old capitals in Japan. Located near Lake Biwa.
naginata	A weapon, best described as a spear tipped with a sword blade.
Onjôji Temple	Also known as Miidera Temple.
rônin	Samurai without masters. Often served as mercenaries.
Saegusa	A family name which may also be spelled and pronounced as Saigusa.
seppuku	This is the same as hara-kiri, or ritual suicide.
Shiragi Myôjin	Myôjin means a kind-hearted god – "the kind-hearted god Shiragi."
Shugo	Provincial constable; later military governor.
Tôkyô	Prior to the Meiji period (1867), the town was called Edo.

APPENDIX 2 - NOTABLE PERSONALITIES

Minamoto (Hemi) Yoshikiyo (1075-1149)

Third son of Shinrasaburô Yoshimitsu, born in the Shiga palace in Ômi. As a child he was given the name Onkômaru. His mother is unknown. He died on the 23rd of July, but one source states it was 1145, not 1149. Yoshikiyo used also the name Gyôbusaburô. Yoshikiyo was originally in Hitachi with his father, and it is from this area that the name Takeda first appears. It was in Yoshida district at a village called Takeda that Yoshikiyo finally ended up, and the villagers later called him Takeda kanja. After being accused of a crime Yoshikiyo and his son Kiyomitsu were sent to Ichikawa village in Kai. Yoshikiyo was later pardoned and given the post as Gesu shiki over Ichikawa village - a kind of local administrator. A manor was built in the area of Ichikawa Daimon village, and it was from here that the Takeda power and influence gradually expanded. Later the Takeda moved to the Hemi area in Koma district.

Minamoto (Hemi) Kiyomitsu (1110-1168)

The first-born son of Yoshikiyo. According to the source 'Takeda keizu' he was born at the Hirashio mansion in Ichikawa in Kai on June 19th. But another, more reliable source states that he was born at the Takeda village in Hitachi. His mother is said to have been the daughter of Minamoto Kanemune. Together with his father he moved from Hirashio to their new mansion in Wakamiko in the Koma district in 1130. Gradually the Takeda expanded their influence to the Yatsuga-take mountain ranges. Since he lived in the Hemi area he adopted the name Hemi Tarô, but went also by the name Hemi kanja. In 1151 he erected the Dôjôshinritsuji temple to the Shingon sect of Buddhism. According to the 'Takeda keizu' Kiyomitsu passed away on June 8th 1168 at his Tanido castle.

Takeda Ariyoshi (?-1200)

His father was Takeda Nobuyoshi. Ariyoshi also used the name Sabeenojô. In 1180 when Minamoto Yoritomo rallied what supporters he could for his rebellion against Taira Ariyoshi, his brethren Ichijô Tadayori, Itagaki Kanenobu, Takeda (Isawa) Nobumitsu and their father joined Yoritomo's side. Ariyoshi took part in the rebellion of Kajiwara Kagetoki in 1200. He died on the 25th of August the same year.

Takeda Ujinobu (?-1394)

His father was Takeda Nobutake. He also went by the names Takeda Jirô and Nobushige. He held the titles *Daizendayû*, Izu *no Kami* and Hyûga *no Kami*. He held the post as *jitô* of

Hagari village, and also held the title Shugo of Kai. Takeda Ujinobu is said to have been an eager supporter of Buddhism and sponsored several temples. He died on June 13th 1394.

Takeda Nobushige (?-1450)

The first born son of Nobumitsu. His mother was the daughter of Oyamada Yasaburô. As a child Nobushige went by the name Saburô. Nobushige's father, Nobumitsu, took part in Uesugi Ujinori's rebellion (*Zenshû no ran*) in 1416, and fled to Mount Kôya (Kôyasan) when he heard his father had committed suicide. Here he shaved his head and took the Buddhist name Kôzôbô. In 1440 at the time of the *Yûki no ran* Nobushige returned to public life. He took part in the attack on Yûki castle and received great praise for his actions. On returning to Kai he set out at once to restore the Takeda family to its rightful place, and in order to do that he challenged and defeated the Atobe family. After accomplishing most of his father's wishes he died in November of 1450.

Takeda Nobutake (?-1359)

Third son of Nobumune. His mother remains unknown. Nobutake also used the names Hikoroku, Saburô and Izu Saburô. He held many titles during his life: Mutsu *no Kami*, Izu *no Kami*, Kai *no Kami*, *Shugo* of Aki, Kai and Wakasa, *Kyûshû tandai*, Hyôgo *no Suke*, Shûri *no Suke*, and Sama *no Suke*. In 1332 he joined the Kantô army on its advance towards Kyôto. It is noted that he used a deep-red colored *saihai* - supposedly a gift from Takauji. In the end of 1335 Nobutake sided with Takauji when the latter gave the call to arms. Nobutake attacked Kumagai Renkaku's Yano castle in Aki on the 26th of December. In January 1336 Nobutake joined Kô Moronao at Seta, and together they held Hachiman Mountain. In June he attacked and captured Fukuda castle in Settsu province. It was after this successful campaign that Nobutake was promoted to *Shugo* of Kai and Wakasa. For the remainder of his life Nobutake was a loyal warrior serving under Ashikaga Takauji. Nobutake was in fact a multi-talented samurai and especially known for his elegant and refined way of behavior - when needed. He was truly skilled in the art of writing *waka* poems. From 1342 until 1345 Nobutake led the construction of temples. After Takauji's death in 1358 Nobutake shaved his head and became a Buddhist priest, dying on July the 13th of the following year (July 1362 according to another source).

Takeda Nobutada (?)

His father was Takeda Nobumitsu. The exact year of his birth and death are unknown. Nobutada was for a period called Osaburô, most likely when he was a child. In 1213, during the rebellion of Wada Yoshimori, Nobutada joined his father and fought alongside the government forces. According to the source Azumakagami Nobutada and his father met with Wada (Asahina) Yoshihide, one of Wada Yoshimori's sons. Azumakagami claims that Wada Yoshihide lost the heart to fight and fled from the field. In the Jôkyû rebellion of 1219 an incident that led to distrust between father and son occurred. This distrust followed their relationship for the remainder of their lives. After this rebellion there is little reported about Nobutada's further actions and activities.

Takeda Nobutoki (?-1289)

His father was Takeda Nobumasa. Nobutoki also used the name and title Gorojirô, Izu *no Kami*. He was granted the title *Shugo* of Aki and it is believed that he held the position between 1264 and 1275. He died in 1289.

His father was Takeda Nobumitsu. Nobunaga used the names Rokurô and Ichijô Rokurô. He took part in the Genpei War and was renowned for his bravery. He also made a name for himself as a skilled archer. The last time his name is mentioned is in the year 1223, in connection with an archery ceremony. There is no information on his death.

Takeda Nobunaga (1389-1457)

His father was Takeda Nobumitsu. Nobunaga also used the name Uma *no Suke*. After his father's death in 1417 he hid from the Kamakura warriors who sought him, and for a time fled to a neighboring province. In 1421 Nobunaga returned to Kai to try to rescue his son and challenge the Atobe clan. The Kamakura government sent an envoy named Yoshimi Norinao to Kai to investigate Nobunaga's activities. In 1425 an army under the command of Uesugi Fusazane (other source Mochizane) invaded Kai province in search of Nobunaga, but met with no success. Kamakura tried again in 1426, in fact twice more, before eventually defeating Nobunaga. He was taken to Kamakura as a hostage. After serving the Kamakura government he escaped in 1433 and made his way back to Kai. His forces were defeated at the battle at Arakawa, and he was forced to make his way to Suruga, with his enemies in pursuit. Sources are a little unclear on what happened next, but he eventually returned to Kai and challenged the Atobe family. He took part in putting down the Yûki rebellion of 1440 and was praised for his actions. In 1456 he marched towards Kazusa and after defeating rebellions was rewarded with the position of *Shugo* of Kazusa. He settled down in Chônan and Marigayatsu, and died in 1457.

Takeda Nobuharu (?-1413)

His father was Takeda Ujinobu (Nobushige). He used the name Shûri *no Suke* and the titles Mutsu *no Kami* and Izu *no Kami*. He also held the position of *Shugo* of Kai. A note from 1352 in the source Taheiki refers to Ujinobu's son, Shûri *no Suke* Nobuharu, taking part in actions under Ashikaga Takauji. The following year he was in the army that marched on Kyôto. Another note on him can be found in a letter at the Daizenji temple. Here it is written that in 1355, on the 21st of April, Nobuharu, who supported the northern Court, challenged followers of the southern Court within the province. He set up camp at Kashiwao Mountain in Kai, and defeated the invaders under the command of Yoshino Tomonori. Soon after this victory he was forced to deal with rebellion behind his own lines. The Isawa family was once again causing trouble and letters to the Daizenji reveal that he prayed to the gods for help in defeating his enemies. These are letters dated 1355 and 1365. It is believed he took over the post as *Shugo* in 1373, but another source states 1376. Before this time the family mansion had been in Isawa, but after trouble broke out Nobuharu Nobushige found it best to move, and built a castle at Senno in Shioyama village. In a rebellion by the Hemi family in 1413 the castle of Senno was captured, and Nobuharu is said to have fled to the Hagiwara Mountains. He remained at Yanagisawa, dying on October 23rd of the same year. (There are different reports as to the month and year in which he died, but this is the generally accepted date).

Takeda Nobumasa (?-1265)

Takeda (Isawa) Nobumitsu's third son. Nobumasa also used the name Takeda Shôgorô. According to one source his mother came from the Utsunomiya family. It is said that due to a false charge Nobumasa was first banished to Aki province. But he was supposedly later pardoned and given titles as Lord over Izu, Wakasa, and Aki provinces, but this information is difficult to verify. He was recorded as one of 16 competitors in a *yabusame* tournament in August of 1195. In 1219 his name appears on a list of soldiers that followed Fujiwara Yoritsune when he was ordered to the Kantô area. In 1221 he took part in the campaign against the Emperor in Kyôto. In June of 1235 Takeda Nobumasa joined in with the Rokuhara army in the quelling of a military conflict between religious followers from the Kôfukuji temple and the Sekishôsui shrine. Nobumasa passed away on January 6th 1265.

Takeda (Isawa) Nobumitsu (1162-1248)

Nobumitsu was the fifth of five sons, his father being Takeda Nobuyoshi. He also went by the name Isawa Gorô. Along with his father he took part in the Genpei wars (1180-85). In January of 1184 he joined Minamoto Noriyori in the campaign against Kiso Yoshinaka. After his brother and father lost their territories Nobumitsu was granted their lands. In August of 1200 his older brother, Ariyoshi, died and Nobumitsu was named heir. At this time he went by the name Isawa Gorô, but soon after changed it to Takeda Nobumitsu. Later Nobumitsu took part in the Ano Zenjô rebellion and later in 1213 the Wada Yoshimori rebellion. On both occasions he joined the Minamoto side. In 1221 he was one of the commanders of the Tôsandô army that advanced on Kyôto. Evidence from that time indicates he was promoted to *Shugo* of Aki. He was also well known for his skills in the way of the bow and was therefore nicknamed one of the "Four Heavenly Kings." In fact, records show that he came in second during an archery tournament held on August 16th 1245. He became a Buddhist priest toward the end of his life and changed his name to Izu Nyûdô Kôren. He was also given the title Izu *no Kami*. He died on the 19th of August 1248 (other sources indicate December 5th).

Takeda Nobumitsu (?-1417)

His father was Takeda Nobuharu. He was also called Jirô. He used the titles Aki *no Kami* and *Akinyûdô*. It is unclear whether he was the second or the first-born son of Nobuharu, but sources tend to agree he was the second-born. At his *genpuku* ceremony it is believed he received permission to use a character from the *Shôgun*, Ashikaga Yoshimitsu. He played an important part in the Zenshû-no-ran in 1416. The rebellion was a lost cause and in 1417 a Kamakura general named Uesugi Norimune invaded Kai and forced Nobumitsu to run, ending up at Mount Tokusa. At this mountain fortress Nobumitsu committed seppuku on the 6th of February.

Takeda Nobumoto (?)

Another of Takeda Nobuharu's sons. In the Zenshû rebellion of 1416 he joined his brother Nobumitsu. They were defeated in the battle by forces from Echigo and Shinano, and Nobumoto returned to Kai province. When he heard of his brother's suicide he fled to Mount Kôya where he tried to lie low for a time by shaving his head and becoming a Buddhist priest. The government in Kyôto gave him the title of *Shugo* of Kai in 1417. He returned to Kai, but time and time again he had to receive help from the Ogasawara family in Shinano to quell rebellion in Kai province. This hectic life took its toll, and he died young in 1421 (or 1426).

Nobuyoshi was born on the 15th of August in Hemi mansion. His father was the famous Minamoto Kiyomitsu. Sources differ on whether he was Kiyomitsu's first or second son, and also state that Kiyomitsu had twins. In his first years he went by the name Ryûkômaru, but later he used the name Takeda Tarô. After his father moved to the villages of Amari and Kagami the Takeda village was left to Nobuyoshi. He built a mansion on a hill on the right bank of the Kamanashi River - today a monument can be seen at the site. He took part in the Genpei wars (1180-85) on Minamoto Yoritomo's side. During the wars he hunted for Taira followers in the provinces of Shinano and Suruga, and was promoted to *Shugo* of Suruga. He took part in many battles in the western part of Honshû, but by the end of the Genpei wars Nobuyoshi's popularity marked him as a potential enemy of the Shôgun. In 1184 his son, Ichijô Tadayori, was murdered in Kamakura on orders from Minamoto Yoritomo. After this display of power Yoritomo stripped Nobuyoshi of his official positions, demonstrating his power over the Takeda lord. Nobuyoshi died on March the 9th, 1186.

The following list shows which Takeda lords held the post of Shugo of Kai from 1331 until 1573.

1331	until	1333	Takeda Masayoshi (Isawa Masayoshi)
1333	until	?	?
?	until	1336	Takeda Masayoshi (Isawa Masayoshi)
?	until	?	?
1351	until	1359	Takeda Nobutake (Aki Takeda line)
1359	until	1368	Takeda Nobushige
1368	until	1373	?
1373	until	1385	Takeda Nobuharu
1385	until	?	?
?	until	1394	Takeda Nobushige (Ujinobu)
?	until	?	?
?	until	1417	Takeda Nobumitsu
1418	until	1419	Takeda Nobumoto (it is also recorded that he took office in 1417)
1419	until	1423	?
1423	until	1450	Takeda Nobushige
1450	until	1455	Takeda Nobumori
1455	until	1466	Takeda Nobumasa
1466	until	?	?
1494	until	1507	Takeda Nobutsuna (one source states that Nobutsuna took over in 1505)
1507	until	1541	Takeda Nobutora
1541	until	1573	Takeda Shingen (also held the post as Shugo of Shinano)
1573	until	?	Takeda Katsuyori (also held the post as Shugo of Shinano)

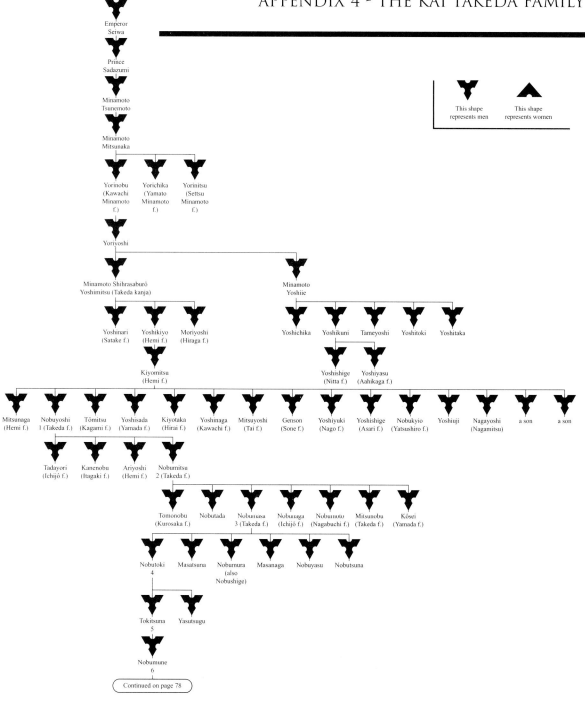

This shape represents men

This shape represents women

Emperor Seiwa

Prince Sadazumi

Minamoto Tsunemoto

Minamoto Mitsunaka

Yorinobu (Kawachi Minamoto f.) Yorichika (Yamato Minamoto f.) Yorinitsu (Settsu Minamoto f.)

Yoriyoshi

Minamoto Shihrasaburô Yoshimitsu (Takeda kanja)   Minamoto Yoshiie

Yoshinari (Satake f.) Yoshikiyo (Hemi f.) Moriyoshi (Hiraga f.)   Yoshichika Yoshikuni Tameyoshi Yoshitoki Yoshitaka

Kiyomitsu (Hemi f.)   Yoshishige (Nitta f.) Yoshiyasu (Aahikaga f.)

Mitsunaga (Hemi f.) Nobuyoshi 1 (Takeda f.) Tômitsu (Kagami f.) Yoshisada (Yamada f.) Kiyotaka (Hirai f.) Yoshinaga (Kawachi f.) Mitsuyoshi (Tai f.) Genson (Sone f.) Yoshiyuki (Nago f.) Yoshishige (Asari f.) Nobukyio (Yatsushiro f.) Yoshiuji Nagayoshi (Nagamitsu) a son a son

Tadayori (Ichijô f.) Kanenobu (Itagaki f.) Ariyoshi (Hemi f.) Nobumitsu 2 (Takeda f.)

Tomonobu (Kurosaka f.) Nobutada Nobumasa 3 (Takeda f.) Nobunaga (Ichijô f.) Nobumoto (Nagabuchi f.) Mitsunobu (Takeda f.) Kôsei (Yamada f.)

Nobutoki 4 Masatsuna Nobumura (also Nobushige) Masanaga Nobuyasu Nobutsuna

Tokitsuna 5 Yasutsugu

Nobumune 6

Continued on page 78

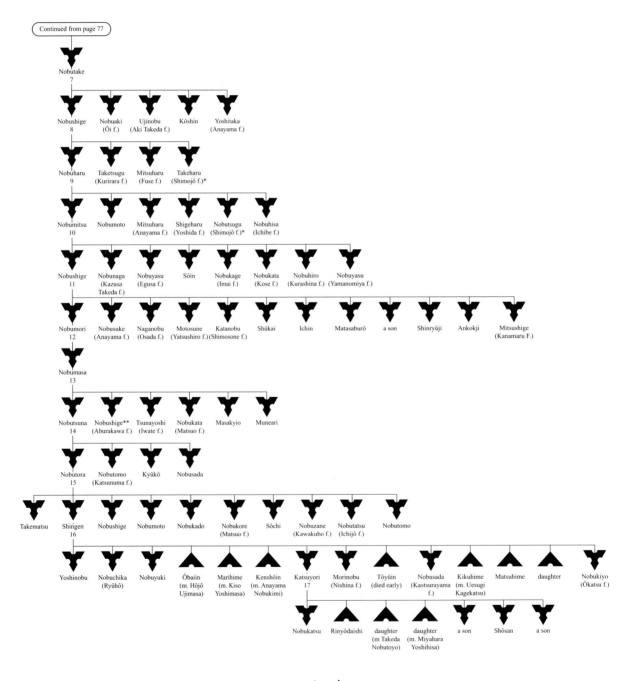

Continued from page 77

Nobutake
7

Nobushige 8 · Nobuaki (Ōi f.) · Ujinobu (Aki Takeda f.) · Kōshin · Yoshitaka (Anayama f.)

Nobuharu 9 · Taketsugu (Kurirara f.) · Mitsuharu (Fuse f.) · Takeharu (Shimojō f.)*

Nobumitsu 10 · Nobumoto · Mitsuharu (Anayama f.) · Shigeharu (Yoshida f.) · Nobutsugu (Shimojō f.)* · Nobuhisa (Ichibe f.)

Nobushige 11 · Nobunaga (Kazusa Takeda f.) · Nobuyasu (Egusa f.) · Sōin · Nobukage (Imai f.) · Nobukata (Kose f.) · Nobuhiro (Kurashina f.) · Nobuyasu (Yamanomiya f.)

Nobumori 12 · Nobusuke (Anayama f.) · Naganobu (Osada f.) · Motosune (Yatsushiro f.) · Katanobu (Shimosone f.) · Shūkai · Ichin · Matasaburō · a son · Shinryūji · Ankokji · Mitsushige (Kanamaru F.)

Nobumasa 13

Nobutsuna 14 · Nobushige** (Aburakawa f.) · Tsunayoshi (Iwate f.) · Nobukata (Matsuo f.) · Masakyio · Muneari

Nobutora 15 · Nobutomo (Katsunuma f.) · Kyūkō · Nobusada

Takematsu · Shingen 16 · Nobushige · Nobumoto · Nobukado · Nobukore (Matsuo f.) · Sōchi · Nobuzane (Kawakubo f.) · Nobutatsu (Ichijō f.) · Nobutomo

Yoshinobu · Nobuchika (Ryūhô) · Nobuyuki · Ôbaiin (m. Hôjô Ujimasa) · Marihime (m. Kiso Yoshimasa) · Kenshôin (m. Anayama Nobukimi) · Katsuyori 17 · Morinobu (Nishina f.) · Tôyûin (died early) · Nobusada (Kastsurayama f.) · Kikuhime (m. Uesugi Kagekatsu) · Matsuhime · daughter · Nobukiyo (Ôkatsu f.)

Nobukatsu · Rinyôdaishi · daughter (m Takeda Nobutoyo) · daughter (m. Miyahara Yoshihisa) · a son · Shôsan · a son

SOURCES
(All in Japanese)

Buki to Bôgu Nihonhen. By Toda Tôsei, Shinkigensha 1998.

Kai Takeda shi. By Ueno Haruo, Shinjinbutsu ôraisha 1972.

Kakei. By Toyoda Takeshi, Tokyodô shuppan 1978.

Kamakura - Muromachi jinmei jiten. Shinjinbutsu ôraisha 1990.

Nihon kassen zuten. By Sasama Yoshihiko, Yûsankaku 1997.

Nihon no meizoku 5. Shinjinbutsu ôraisha 1989.

Rekishi gunzô series nr 5, 10, 13, 37. Gakken Tokyo.

Rekishi to tabi 6 - Sengoku daimyô-ke no hasshô to yukari no chi. Akita shoten 1999.

Sengoku daimyô keifu jinmei jiten - higashi-hen. Shinjinbutsu ôraisha 1985.

Sengoku kassen daijiten 3. Shinjinbutsu ôraisha 1989.

Sengoku kassen manual. By Tôgô Ryû, Kodansha 2001.

Shugo - Sengoku daimyô jiten. By Nishigaya Yasuhiro, Tokyodô shuppan 1998.

Takeda ichizoku no subete. Shinjinbutsu ôraisha 1998.

Takeda Nobushige. By Isogai Masayoshi 1974.

Takeda Shingen no subete. Shinjinbutsu ôraisha 1978.

Takeda Shingen sono karei naru keifu. By Sakamoto Tokuichi, Akita shoten 1988.

Teihon - Takeda Shingen. By Isogai Masayoshi, Shinjinbutsu ôraisha 1977.

Yamanashi-ken no rekishi. Yamakawa shuppansha, Tokyo 1999.

Upcoming titles in the Saga of the Samurai series

Book #2
Saga of the Samurai: Takeda Nobutora - The Kai Takeda 2
(1494-1574)

Book 2 describes the Takeda during the Ônin War and follows the life of Takeda Nobutora and his unification of Kai. With sixteen pages of color plates, maps, and illustrations, this book continues the amazing story of the Kai Takeda and their remarkable history.

Book #3
Saga of the Samurai: Takeda Shingen - The Kai Takeda 3
(1521-1548)

Book 3 in this series tells the story of Shingen's early years, including his military and diplomatic relations with the Suwa, Murakami, Ogasawara, and Imagawa families. Sixteen pages of color plates, maps, and illustrations paint a vivid image of Shingen's life during these years.

For more information and comments on the Saga of the Samurai series, be sure to visit

WWW.SAGAOFTHESAMURAI.COM